Six Stages
of
Forgiving
Others

Six Stages

of

Forgiving Others

A SPIRIT-LED ADVENTURE

Georg Karl

Pleasant Word
PW A Division of WinePress Group

Pleasant Word (a division of WinePress Publishing, PO Box 428, Enumclaw, WA 98022) functions only as book publisher. As such, the ultimate design, content, editorial accuracy, and views expressed or implied in this work are those of the author.

Unless otherwise noted, all Scriptures are taken from the *Holy Bible, New International Version®, NIV®*. Copyright © 1973, 1978, 1984 by Biblica, Inc.™ Used by permission of Zondervan. All rights reserved worldwide.

ISBN 13: 978-1-4141-1435-4
ISBN 10: 1-4141-1435-4
Library of Congress Catalog Card Number: 2009903168

To Jeanne,

my wife,

my partner in life and ministry.

Your affirmation gave me the courage to write.

Contents

In Appreciation

I AM VERY grateful to my readers, Susan Broerman and Beth Davis, whose feedback on my manuscripts and keen insights taught me how to express ideas in writing.

I deeply appreciate the First Church of God family, with whom I share in the life of discipleship and who supported me in ministry for over two decades.

Dear Beth,
You have served the
Lord in so many ways
and your work on
this book will always
be in my ix life. Thank you,
pus Keol

SECTION ONE

HOPE -
FOR THOSE WHO
WANT TO FORGIVE
OTHERS

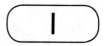

A Living Portrait of Forgiveness

I S IT POSSIBLE to forgive those who hurt us most and truly be free of crippling anger? When only God can create the forgiving heart we lack, dare we depend on God to do so? Can we forgive when someone deprives us of our life's greatest hopes, such as a secure marriage, a house and home, innocence, or even an only child? Is God's work within us sufficient and consistent enough to sustain our decision to forgive those who hurt us deeply? This is a true story that will answer these questions.

During my junior year of high school, I had grown cold toward God and moved far from a life for Christ that began with spiritual revivals in my church's youth group. The spiritual decline occurred gradually and there was nothing tangible to alert me to any spiritual danger, for I lived well within positive social and moral boundaries. While working at the supermarket one night stocking shelves after store hours, I joined in the all-male crew's swaggering chorus of obscenities. Hearing it come out of my own mouth disturbed my still-responsive conscience.

I was ashamed. After work that night, I knelt in my bedroom and asked God for forgiveness and renewal. I recommitted my life to Christ and began a fresh walk with Him.

The next day in my auto-shop class, I worked with a fellow student whom I hadn't previously met. He was not ashamed of Christ and didn't take long to ask, "Have you been born again?" In the mid-1970s, that was the popular way to ask about another's relationship with Christ. Eager to take a clear stand for Christ, I gladly reported my own renewed allegiance to the Savior and said, "Yes, I am."

We exchanged stories and Alan immediately shifted the conversation to matters of biblical doctrine about which he thought we might not see eye-to-eye. Since we didn't attend the same church, he found a point of discussion about a particular difference of belief. Alan had a clear advantage because he was a Baptist minister's son and a Bible-quiz champion! He accurately quoted scriptures I barely recognized without looking them up. His knowledge of Scripture instantly motivated me to begin studying my own Bible.

Despite those few differences, from that time forward, we developed a close friendship that grew over the next two years. Alan led me to an unwavering love for Jesus Christ and His Word. God placed him in my life at just the right time so that I might become a strong disciple of Christ rather than a perpetual spiritual beginner. We played basketball (and he always won), talked about Scripture, and encouraged each other in our growing faith.

A CHRISTIAN LEADER IN THE MAKING

Alan was an amazing young person and I recognized his extraordinary qualities even at the age of seventeen. The only child of a ministerial couple, Dr. Charles and Audrey Littman, Alan was a preacher and evangelist both at his father's church and at Youth for Christ rallies. When he wasn't preaching, he served as an usher at the church or in a variety of other capacities. People came to Christ when he spoke and grew closer to Christ when he befriended them. Someone might think that being so involved at church would make him socially dull or odd, but he was just as popular at school and highly respected as student manager of the varsity boys' basketball team. Alan was an inspiration to both young and old. He was remarkable.

The Littman family often included me in their loving home. Rev. and Mrs. Littman lived out the scriptures in daily life and supported Alan in memorizing them. At age six he had fallen in love with the scriptures and the Savior whom those same scriptures proclaim.[1] His mother would review his Scripture memory verses and the "Quiz-Time" questions and answers each morning at breakfast. At one point, Alan had flawlessly committed to memory the New Testament books of Galatians, Ephesians, Philippians, and Colossians.

It was clear to me that God would use Alan as a significant leader in the church, most likely as a successful pastor or evangelist. I, for one, would have wanted to listen to his sermons. The director of a local Christian youth ministries organization, Don Glaske, said that Alan was "a handsome guy, immaculately clean, polite, liked everyone and liked in return, good sense of humor even on himself, an achiever, beyond his years."[2] I could only add that he was a very good athlete, had an energizing personality, was a natural leader, and would be considered an asset to any community. I had no doubt that he would become one of my generation's greatest Christian leaders. Mine is not a unique assessment but a common one among the many who knew him then. He graduated from high school in June 1977, full of promise and ambition. One can only imagine what joy and pride he brought to his parents.

UNIMAGINABLE TRAGEDY

The people who arrived for worship at the First Baptist Church in St. Joseph, Michigan, on Sunday morning, July 16, 1978, were informed of a heartrending tragedy concerning the only child of their pastoral couple. During the night, Alan had been shot and killed at the supermarket where he was employed. Rev. and Mrs. Littman had been informed by the state police officers about their missing son's fate at 8:00 that morning.[3] It was a heinous, premeditated assault, which horrified the small city in southwestern Michigan. It had been over two years since high school and my friendships had migrated to new college relationships, so I had not seen Alan or his parents. I found out about the tragedy, like everyone else in the city, through the local newspaper. I was stunned and speechless.

The hardest part about attending the viewing was seeing his parents. I knew how their son's life gave them assurance of their own hopeful future; after all, children represent that to most parents. When I saw Mrs. Littman, she told me that during the previous weeks, Alan had been thinking about calling me just to reconnect and renew our friendship. I only wish that meeting had happened. Still, my mind was on how his parents would move forward from this horrendous tragedy. It would only be human to feel anger due to this awful and entirely senseless loss in their life.

TRIAL AND JUDGMENT

The following nine months were consumed with the drama of a full-scale investigation, witnesses, arrests, trials, jury deliberations, a conviction, and a life sentence imposed on the assailant. The entire incident was published in the newspaper, exposing all the gruesome details of the murder as they were uncovered. The community couldn't escape the reminders of how senselessly one of her finest sons was taken. All of the reporting simply served only to magnify the Littmans' nightmare.

The trial revealed the merciless manner of Alan's murder, all for the assailant's fleeting financial gain of $16,000 in cash. Ironically, the cash itself led to the arrest because the bank had record of the sequential serial numbers of the bills.[4] Afterward, the assailant's wife was also charged and convicted as an accomplice.

The mandatory life sentence was imposed by Judge Byrns on April 13, 1979.[5] The judge explained to the murderer, "I'm taking steps so you die in prison and are never released into society again."[6] He poignantly expressed the sentiments of the community, except for those who may have preferred an execution. He added, "About the only forgiveness you can get is Divine because society can never forgive you."[7] That seemed a fair assumption.

AN UNEXPECTED TURN

Punishment never resolves a hurt in anyone's mind. The wrongdoing that hurts us most has a life of its own and begins to consume everything as long as unforgiveness persists. Rev. and Mrs. Littman knew the peril of an unforgiving heart. They knew the hurt of their son's loss could eat them alive, cripple their fruitful ministry, and strip them of joy. They knew the only path to victory over this devastating wrong was the way of the cross. There, God enables us to forgive as only He can.

Within the weeks following the murder, Rev. and Mrs. Littman made the decision to forgive the assailant and shared that decision publicly with their congregation. This was a bold step of faith that was entirely unexpected if not incomprehensible. The news about the Littmans' forgiveness of the assailant spread quickly throughout the community. The idea of the parents' forgiveness impacted those who heard about it even more so than the news of the murder. Crimes of this nature are senselessly repeated in our society, but forgiveness of this magnitude is precious and rare. Didn't the judge say, "Society can never forgive you"? How could more be expected of Alan's parents? Yet they did what seemed humanly impossible: they forgave the one who hurt them most. By that act, Rev. and Mrs. Littman were set free from a life sentence of their own. They were set free for a future life of friendships, faith, and laughter. Though they would always long for Alan, they could anticipate a heavenly reunion with him.

ABUNDANT LIVING

Rev. Littman was reunited with his son twenty-five years later, when he slipped away from life to Glory on August 21, 2003, at age 71. He had continued in ministry, in his love for people and music, and in his shared life with his wife, Audrey. Some years after the Littmans left St. Joseph, he wrote a testimony titled "We've Picked Up the Pieces." He wrote that when Alan was taken from them, their "world stopped" and "completely fell apart." They couldn't pray, cry, praise the Lord, or even think. "Nothing mattered, nothing was important."[8]

After such an injurious wound, is God's grace sufficient to restore peace and implant mercy for the one who inflicted the pain? Dr. Littman wrote, "God can and He does give perfect peace. We've picked up the pieces and have found God is good and He is faithful as He promised. We are living proof that His grace is sufficient."[9] In fact, he writes:

By God's grace, and only by God's grace, we harbor no bitterness or hate in our hearts. We are praying that the one now serving a life sentence without parole for first degree premeditated murder would come to know

Jesus Christ as Saviour and Lord. One of the greatest reunions would be for him to meet Alan some day.[10]

Of course there were down days through which the Littmans were buoyed by the words of a familiar song:[11] "There's not a friend like the lowly Jesus. No, not one! No, not one! No night so dark but his love can cheer us. No, not one! No, not one! Jesus knows all about our struggles; He will guide till the day is done…" Even five years after her husband went to be with the Lord, Mrs. Littman expressed the ongoing grace of God, which sustains us when we forgive. She wrote, "We were only able to get through the situation and go on without being bitter and unforgiving with the help of Christ who gives us the strength and the power to do all things."[12] Her life continues to be filled with friendships, joy, and faith, and it demonstrates Jesus' promise in John 10:10: "I have come that they may have life, and have it to the full."

Yes, God can and does make forgiving those who hurt us a real possibility. Forgiving others is a gift of grace that enables one to live out the call of Christ: "Freely you have received, freely give."[13] Forgiving those who hurt us most enables us to receive God's grace, for Jesus taught us to pray, "Forgive us our debts as we also have forgiven our debtors."[14] The other alternative will make even the most fun-loving personality become unattractively harsh and critical. God's will is that mercy would follow us all the days of our lives.[15] Forgiving others maintains a merciful heart and is made possible by a merciful God. "The one who calls you is faithful and He will do it."[16] God may grow the forgiveness quickly and miraculously, as is the Littmans' continuing testimony, or slowly and arduously as others experience. In whichever manner God grows it, forgiveness for those who hurt us most is entirely possible. For "what is impossible with men is possible with God."[17]

Forgiving others sets us free for abundant life. Unforgiveness confines our divinely designed personality. Forgiving others sets us free from being consumed by bitterness and hate. Forgiving others is what every Christian is commissioned and authorized to do. "If you forgive anyone his sins, they are forgiven; if you do not forgive them, they are not forgiven" (John 20:23). The following pages will lead to an understanding of forgiveness and a plan for how one can grant it to those who hurt us deeply. God makes forgiving others a possibility, and each person is invited to experience its liberation.

The Meaning of Forgiveness

THE MEANING OF the phrase "I forgive you" may appear to be subject to individual interpretation, but in reality, it is not. Forgiveness is not as beauty is to the eye of the beholder. Beauty is subjective and based upon cultural norms and personal preferences; forgiveness is far more objective.

If forgiveness were subject to the definition of the one offering it, the recipient would never be quite sure about the future of that relationship. A woman might say, "I forgive you," but will her statement hold true when she needs some relational leverage later? A man might have said, "I forgive you," but why does the "forgiven" wife feel she has been paying off some invisible debt by walking on eggshells around him for the past ten years? Sometimes the words "I forgive you" really mean that the offense in question has been placed in accounts receivable. The phrase is really whispering, *I'll let you make it up to me if you can.* At other times those words mean, *I'll put the offense on the back burner of my mind.* Then there's the definition that really means someone is simply willing to be eaten alive by the hurt and won't say anything about it directly; their silent suffering shouts out how they really feel. So, when the words "I forgive you" are spoken, what do they really mean, what actually occurs, and what can we expect?

No matter what people think they mean when they offer forgiveness, the good news is that the true meaning of forgiveness is not subject to the person saying the words. Forgiveness is objective. Forgiveness is a cleansing for both the forgiver and the forgiven. Forgiveness can never mean that the offense is placed on the back burner, in accounts receivable, or all over the face of the silently suffering martyr.

Often it helps to use different words to remove the emotions associated with common phrase. The words "I forgive you" are usually associated with a reprieve from punishment but that association is too narrow. Forgiveness must mean something more than "I won't punish you" for it to transform our relationships and us. We need another phrase to help us understand the meaning of forgiveness objectively.

FORGIVENESS SEPARATES US FROM HURTFUL FAILURE

Our failures are chained to us until we are released by forgiveness. How would the phrase "I release you from what you did" affect us if we heard it spoken when we needed to be forgiven? When we have offended someone, we are identified by that relational failure until that person releases us from it. That release is forgiveness. When someone forgives, he is releasing us from the offense with which we were identified and for which we are blamed. You see, forgiveness is a release and a separation of the offending person from the actual act of sin. In other words, release and separation are at the core of what the Bible means by forgiveness.

The Meaning of Forgiveness

The Greek word translated *forgive* in the Lord's Prayer is αφιημι and is used 133 times in the New Testament. Of all the words that may be translated as *forgive*, this is the most common. While forty-seven of those instances are translated *forgive*, that same Greek word is used fifty-eight times with the meaning *to leave or depart from a group of people*. This is the same Greek word used when Jesus departs from a crowd. So, separating one from another is the core idea behind both departing from a scene and forgiving a sin. Being forgiven is like saying good-bye to that offense because we are released from our identity with it. True forgiveness completely separates the offender from the offense—the spiritual or moral failure, the sin, in which he or she has been involved.

Release and separation define forgiveness. When we forgive, we are saying, "I release and separate you from the cause of my hurt." We are disassociating the offending person from the pain inflicted on us. When we release the person who hurt us, the offense no longer restricts our freedom to trust, even if some legal relationship is forfeited.

For example, when a marriage ends in divorce, a heavy load of mistrust has built up from numerous bouts of "offensive maneuvers" that may even include infidelity. It is easy to understand why a person would say, "I can't trust him," or, "I'll never trust her again." The legal relationship may be changed but the bond to the couple's children must remain intact. It becomes necessary to trust each other again in the matter of highest value to each, the children's well-being and future. When distrust is absolute, every time the ex-spouse has charge of the children, the one waiting experiences a temporary insanity. In extreme cases, the only resolution the embittered spouse might see is to bring about a murderous end, including the children. Such tragedies frequently play themselves out all through the nightly news both in full and in lesser degrees.

Perhaps the divorce is justified, but when joint custody or visitation rights are legally granted, forgiveness must be sufficient to restore trust for the children's sake. One man whose marriage ended in the wake of several relational failures, including infidelity, forgave his wife and became free enough to acknowledge, "She's become a great mother. She loves my kids and I want them to be around her." Apparently, her level of responsibility improved during the months prior to the divorce. Without forgiving, the whole person is defined by the sin against the marriage, and the possibility of loving parenthood is not even considered.

Once forgiven, a person has a whole new identity with us. That is why forgiveness is transformational. A new and wonderful identity with God is made possible by forgiveness. Conversely, a new and wonderful identity with us is made possible for those who have hurt us when we forgive them.

If we do not release people from their act of offense, then we will find ourselves separated from that person who needs our forgiveness. Which would be preferable to lose, the relationship or the offense? Sadly, many choose to lose the relationship. If one does not release others from an offense, both the offender and the offended will live with it until death do them part. The failure will define the future of the relationship. The choice to not release others from their fault is a spiritual failure itself and holds eternal consequences.

FORGIVENESS ENABLES TIME TO HEAL

Release and separation are the essence of forgiveness throughout the Bible. King David captures the core meaning of forgiveness in several of the psalms, but none relate the meaning better than Psalm 103. Here, in summary about God, David states, "…who forgives all your sins…" (Psalm 103:2). Then, in very picturesque language, David describes forgiveness as an infinite separation of the sinner from the sin. "...as far as the east is from the west, so far has he removed our transgressions from us" (Psalm 103:12).

Imagine this concept on a linear plane. One can travel east or west indefinitely and immeasurably increase the distance between the two with time. When God forgives, He sends us in one direction and our sins in the other direction, moving away from each other indefinitely (see Psalm 103:12). We'll never have to meet that same sin again. We are released and forever separated from that sin. That old sin is nowhere in our vicinity and is less and less able to show itself in our presence with each passing moment. We do not need to fear the time when we will have to again be identified with it before God. That sin is separated from us as far as eastward travels from westward! Forgiveness is infinite separation.

Another image of separation is provided by the prophet Isaiah who said in a prayer, "...you have put all my sins behind your back" (Isaiah 38:17). God sees everything about us, but our confessed sin is not in His view. He has separated our sin from our person by putting our sins behind His back. Now He looks forward and sees us free from that sin with the ability to move forward ourselves. We are released and separated from our sin from God's vantage point.

When we forgive, we regard the person who has wronged us apart from the event that hurt us. We separate the person from the offense so that we appreciate the individual without factoring in their personal failure. As long as that failure continues to condition our regard for him or her, we have not forgiven. When we have separated the failure from the person, we have set that person free to experience our best respect and love.

Even better than setting the offending person free is setting ourselves free by forgiving. As long as we temper our regard for someone by his past failure or offense, we allow ourselves to be governed by that incident. When a hurt in our past determines how we will regard others, it has a governing influence. Without forgiveness, bitterness will take root and poison our inward disposition, our spiritual condition, and everything in our reach. Undeniably then, we need to forgive as much as the offender needs to be forgiven.

Separating the offender from the offense allows healing to begin. After forgiving, time becomes an ally to healing the wound inflicted by the offender. Forgiveness provides growing benefits for every part of the relationship: the person we are forgiving, the condition of the relationship, and the forgiver. Before forgiveness, the hurt is embedded in our memory, and any reminder of that situation brings about a stinging pain.

THE HURT THAT STINGS

Forgiveness takes the stinger out. Imagine being in a closed room with a small group of people engaged in a very important conversation. However, there is an intense awareness of a bumblebee flying around the room. There is the sound of the bee. There is also the sight of the bee. Whenever the sound is heard, one cannot resist looking in that direction because there is a pressing, internal clamoring to know the exact location of that bee. If the location of the bee is near us, then our whole body shifts to sit in a more defensive position. Because of the presence of that bee, the important conversation is ruined. Why? Because that bee has a stinger in it and our awareness of that stinger makes us defensive.

Now, imagine being absolutely convinced that the bumblebee's stinger has been removed. The removal of the stinger was observed and verified. (Please set aside the fact that the bee cannot survive very long after the stinger is removed.) There would still be the sound and sight of the bee; however, the stinger-less bumblebee would not create the defensive posture any longer. We would only be mildly annoyed when the bee flew directly in front of our face, but it would bother us no more than the nuisance of a common housefly. Without the stinger the bee poses no threat.

Forgiveness takes the stinger of hurt from the reminder and memory about the offense we forgave. We may have the memory or encounter a reminder of the hurt, but the memory no longer creates the defensive posture within us. Why? Forgiveness separates the hurtful failure that stings from the one responsible for it. Even if that person is a family member or friend who will always be in our life, either by interaction or recollection, we are set free from being gripped by perpetual defensiveness by separating the offense from the offender. Forgiveness releases that person and separates us from the pain of the past.

The Human Need
to Forgive

HAVE YOU EVER wanted to get away from it all? Most everyone has that desire from time to time. Stress seems to come from every sector of our life. We long to get away from the conflicts at work, in the family, with our children, with people to whom we are connected financially, and even ones at church if the truth were known. So we dream of a solo vacation getaway, all by ourselves, because there is no one with whom we have never known discord. However, not having anyone to share our vacation getaway with also creates turmoil. When we are finally alone, we discover some long-standing internal conflicts about mistakes still left unresolved. To our horror, we discover that the strife is not out there; the battle is within and consumes us from the inside out.

We can get away from people but we cannot avoid ourselves. Even when we're alone, we still fight with the people from whom we have distanced ourselves by hundreds or thousands of miles. The rancor follows us on our vacation. Some of the division and bickering involves people now dead. We feel chained to those damaging relationships and can't find a way to get away from the stress those relationships have caused.

There has only been one way known to humanity for breaking the chains that bind us to life's manifold conflicts—forgiveness. When Jesus mandated forgiveness in the prayer He taught us, He wasn't trying to make life harder. "Forgive us our debts as we also have forgiven our debtors" (Matthew 6:12). Forgiveness was mandated to make life easier! Unforgiven conflict of the past combined with the current conflict of the day always overloads the psychological capacity for managing normal stress. Jesus made the stress load lighter by teaching us to forgive. Human beings need to be proficient at forgiving others.

Apart from offering daily forgiveness, we become subject to the psychiatric maladies, social dysfunctions, and psychological depression caused by the physical and emotional consequences of stress. Stress actually depletes certain chemicals that provide emotional balance. It is no secret that conflict produces such stress. When we are chained to all of the unresolved conflicts in our past and undergo all of the conflicts of the day, we quickly lose our emotional equilibrium! Forgiveness sets us free from conflicts within us and in our past. Karl Menninger, the famed psychiatrist, once said that if he could convince the patients in psychiatric hospitals that their sins were forgiven, seventy-five percent of them could walk out the next day.[18] The same result is true when we forgive.

The human need to forgive others did not escape Jesus' notice, for it is the only demand that is included in the first prayer He taught the new disciples. Why might forgiving others play so crucial a role in the life of faith? If we don't separate people from their past offenses, we forfeit four essential blessings of life. Every human being hungers for these blessings that require us to clear the clutter of conflict by releasing others from their fault.

BLESSING ONE: REGRETS AVOIDED

When we forgive, we avoid living with regrets. The greatest waste of our life is the time—hours, days, months, or even years—we spend embroiled in resentment toward others. An ex-spouse, harsh boss, or exasperating parent can easily consume our best energies and prevent us from achieving our mission or potential in life. We end up regretting the missed opportunity and we blame it on whoever got in the way. Think about how much time, thought, and emotion is given to acting out this hostility in the form of grudges, self-pity, and especially revenge that long outlast the offense. A life can be wasted, positive relationships lost, and potential progress mitigated because revenge actually depletes our personal ambition or love.

Revenge is as weak as hate, which can only destroy. Revenge makes us feel strong but always proves to achieve nothing. Neither does grudge-bearing or self-pity achieve anything positive. Forgiveness is as strong as God's love, which can suffer, redeem, and rise again. Love creates and heals; forgiveness is real strength.

A great relationship lost for a lifetime because of unforgiveness colors the whole of life with regret. A family member who has always been critical of us can drive us away from the church we really want, the reunions we really desire, and the family to which we belong. After years of avoiding that person, we are left with the regrets about what could have been so wonderful. There will be unrealized achievements, of which we were capable, because too much energy was spent on revenge, angry thoughts, and the one-upmanship games with that bitter rival. This disappointment in life's accomplishments leaves us with irreversible regret.

The devil comes to destroy life and would like nothing better for us than to waste the life God gave us.[19] When we amass bitterness and revenge, we play right into the devil's scheming hands. We become drained of the energy and stamina necessary for reaching our God-created potential. For that reason, forgiveness is a survival skill for the pastorate and any other profession that seeks to serve people. Forgiveness is an essential relational skill for reaching the divine possibilities in marriage. Forgiveness prevents the regret of having destroyed the gifts of life that God provides.

I am a pastor, and managing conflicts is the hardest part of my job. Long hours are a badge of honor in my profession. Sharing the good news about Jesus that changes one's eternal destiny is the privilege of ministry. But mediating conflict between people or navigating through conflict with someone wears down even a highly motivated pastor. Discord drains the minister of energy, causes midlife career changes, and drives rising health and life insurance premiums for pastors. Unresolved strife will ruin a ministry and render the minister joyless. If we don't learn to forgive others, our effectiveness diminishes rapidly and our longevity is reduced dramatically.

Pastors and ministers are not spiritual marvels; they are spiritual models. Forgiving others is an essential survival skill for the modern-day pastor and church member alike. Otherwise, we will look back on our life or career, if we can stop blaming others for just a minute, and will see years of unrealized fruitfulness, lost relationships, and forfeited happiness. The thirty-eight year-old's advice is true, "I've learned that when you harbor bitterness, happiness will dock elsewhere."[20] Forgiveness prevents such regret.

BLESSING TWO: RELEASE OF STRESS

Unresolved hurt in our life chains us to the stress-producing conflict that may be as old as twenty years. Those chains of past hurts drain us of energy vitally necessary for today's challenges and relationships. We were not designed to import the stress-producing conflicts from the past, borrow the potential stress-producing discord from tomorrow, and incorporate it all into the normal stress-producing experiences of each day.[21] An unforgiving heart is as anxious about old hurts as it is about new ones. Forgiveness releases us from the chains of unforgiven grievances.

In my pastoral counseling experience, I find that over-stressed people are often chained to the damage done by an expired conflict but do not recognize its continuing impact. Our counseling seeks to release the chains that attach us to those hurts by forgiving others. The opposite of forgiveness is blame, which is the devil's prison guard preventing our release. Blame points us toward revenge and when we plan to get even with someone, we allow that person to continue harming us. As M. Deutsch has said, "Blaming tends to be inflaming."[22] The blame-to-revenge plan is the devil's scheme to defeat us.

Stress is predictable. Doctors Thomas Holmes and Richard Rahe developed a do-it-yourself stress test in 1967. There are 43 stress-producing items on the list, of which over one-third (15) are clearly conflict-related. (More than that are potentially conflict-related.) The conflict-related stress-producing items are assigned 44 percent of the total stress points.[23] These conflicts result in hurts and offenses that take on a life of their own, long past the event which produced them. On top of the stress from the present life experiences, the stress from unforgiven hurts from the past tips the scale against anyone's emotional health.

Forgiveness is the only way known to humanity for stress release. Forgiveness removes the stress of the hurts that either blame or revenge would strap to our backs. Please notice the phrase "stress release." Typically, we hear the phrase "stress relief." Relief from stress can be achieved medically but release cannot. Relief from stress can be achieved by escape through alcohol or drugs, hyper-busy schedules, travel, and constant acquisitions but release cannot be obtained through these means. One can find some relief by displacing the source of conflict, which is what we do, for example, when we displace attention to our difficult marriage with giving our complete attention to our children. Relief is no solution to stress and always leaves us looking back over our shoulder at the ever-present hurt. Release from that conflict-produced stress is realized only by forgiving others.

BLESSING THREE: RESPONSE CONTROL

Unforgiven, painful memories chain us to a harmful stimulus-response pattern that ruins perfectly good relationships. When we refuse to forgive, we also remain defensive against any reminder of the offense by which we were hurt. Human beings were created with physical and emotional reactions that form our defense mechanisms. An unforgiven hurt will cause an involuntary defensive reaction in our emotions and attitude toward any person who shares similar personality traits with the one who hurt us. Still chained to the hurt of the past, the pain needs only a reminder of the original offender to sting us again. Inevitably, we put up our guard when we encounter someone who reminds us of the one who hurt us.

Consider a commonly observed scenario of a child who has developed a grudge against a demeaning father. Although this can happen to a son or a daughter, we'll use a female hypothetical situation for the sake of illustration. As an adult, this daughter with a grudge finds a wonderful man and the relationship blossoms. The two are married and begin to get to know each other in the unique context of marriage. Not long after the marriage has begun, however, the new husband begins to exhibit personality traits similar to her father's.

While a surprise to her, it was not unforeseeable because there are common attributes specific to gender. Still, the pain yielded from her relationship to her father periodically emerges in her emotions by simply being around her new husband. The husband has not hurt her in any way that her father had; the husband only has some similar mannerisms and personality traits, not necessarily the negative ones. The benign similarities still evoke negative emotions associated with her father.

In the course of time, marital disagreements arise. The intensity of these arguments is unjustifiably bitter. The new husband has no idea why he has incurred so much anger. He is not only disagreeing with his wife over particular issues, but unbeknownst to him, he's actually irritating his wife's unhealed childhood emotional wounds. All of the anger due her father is unloaded upon her husband, because to some degree, any man will remind her of her father's offenses until those past emotional wounds heal. That healing requires forgiveness by the adult daughter but she has not yet offered it. Until she does, each normal marital disagreement will incur a volatile reaction that bears the full force of the retaliation toward her childhood hurt.

This young woman's new husband is being asked to pay the price of someone else's failure. In no way did she intend to make her new husband pay for the hurt from her father. It was simply a stimulus-response reaction to some similarity reminiscent of the one who hurt her.

The negative reaction patterns are not limited to family life. Bill Gothard tells about a missionary organization that was trying to understand why the tenure of missionaries was so short.[24] The administrators arranged for someone to interview the missionaries who resigned their assignment. It was discovered that each of those who resigned loved God, were passionate about global missions, and had a deep and abiding sense of call to missionary service. But there was unresolved anger toward a family member with whom the missionary couldn't get along. As young adults, they found themselves in a very close-knit company of missionaries in a foreign country. The young missionaries perceived similarities between their parents and supervisor or between their siblings and colleagues. In some cases, the structural similarity of authority produced an inward angry reaction to any supervision. In other cases, similarity to the personality of siblings produced a defensive response to a colleague.

Forgiving the past offenses against us releases us from a lifetime of reactions that are out of our control and beyond our rational understanding. There are people who are receiving far more than their share of our anger because we are still reacting to some unhealed wound inflicted by another child, a friend, parent, church member, boss, or coworker in our past. Unforgiven offenses hurt as though they were still a live coal from a fire that was thought to be extinguished. It won't go away with time but simply stores up anger to be unleashed upon the next reminder of the offender. Only forgiveness can stop the reproduction of resentment.

Forgiveness enables us to be the master of our responses to various personalities in our life. One person may remind us of another, but forgiveness allows us to give that person a gracious opportunity with us. Forgiving others allows us to be proactive in our relationships. Unforgiveness takes the emotional controls away from us and we become subject to involuntary defensive reactions. If we collect enough grudges, we will soon feel that our life is out of control. Our negative response reactions to similar personalities, mannerisms, or structural authority positions will rob us of becoming the person God intended. God has given us the remedy of forgiveness for involuntary defensive reactions against innocent people.

BLESSING FOUR: SPIRITUAL RENEWAL

Unforgiven hurt prevents the active work of God's grace in our soul and in the church. "See to it that no one misses the grace of God and that no bitter root grows up to cause trouble and defile many" (Hebrews 12:15). The meaning of "bitter root" in this verse is found by contrast with the previous verse "...to live in peace with all men..." (Hebrews 12:14). Bitterness is the opposite of relational peace. It depletes our sensibility and undermines our objectivity about others for it reduces us to one who is "senseless and ignorant."[25] Bitterness is unforgiveness amassed to a destructive quantity; it causes us to miss the grace of God in every relationship.

An end to grudge-bearing is a common mark of the first phase of spiritual revival. The cessation of internal infighting, envy, and vengefulness is a first-fruit of revival and the gateway to more. Reconciliation and forgiveness within the church always precedes the outpouring of the Holy Spirit for we observe that the church at Pentecost was in one accord (Acts 2:1, KJV). That doesn't mean that every person in the church was uniform in thought, but they were unified in a shared relationship to Jesus Christ. Only then was the Holy Spirit poured out on them.

After the church's birth at Pentecost, that unity became possible only by forgiving each other. "Forgive as the Lord forgave you... put on love, which binds them all together in perfect unity" (Colossians 3:13-14). Offenses do occur. Even the early church had sharp disputes (Acts 15:2,39). Forgiving each other was a critical skill for experiencing the fellowship of the Spirit (Philippians 2:1). Unless we release each other from blame, there is no renewal of the church by the Holy Spirit.

Neither can there be personal renewal until we have cleaned out the bitterness "closet." Bitterness and grace cannot share the same space any more than weeds and crops should share the same soil. Forgiving others roots out the bitterness that grows as we rehearse a hurt inflicted upon us. Once bitterness is removed, the renewing grace of God begins to flourish and bear fruit.

Many Christians have found great personal renewal by participating in a spiritual retreat with others. In the fall of 1994, I participated in a Walk to Emmaus retreat. The spiritual renewal among the approximately 40 first-time participants was remarkable. I observed the transformation of resistant and guarded participants into people fully in love with God and openhearted toward brothers in Christ. What happened at that retreat? Of course there were many facets of the weekend that contributed to the renewal, but forgiveness was the impetus that allowed all others to have effect. In many cases, receiving God's forgiveness is what led to renewal. In other cases, renewal of love for God happened when people forgave old grudges.

Serving as a spiritual director in subsequent retreats, I had the opportunity, at the request of the participants, to hear many of the confessions in order to assist in experiencing God's love and forgiveness. A significant number of liberating confessions were about long-term hard feelings toward another person. Anger and bitterness, which had grown without restraint for years or decades, had formed hard-hearted men. Most of these participants had a belief in all the tenants of the Christian faith. Though a person believes the gospel message, unforgiven hurt prevents God's grace from bearing any fruit of love, joy, or peace. Once the pain of past hurts and bitter revenge were confessed as sin and fully exposed to the healing of the Holy Spirit, God quickly transformed years of anger into observable expressions of peace.

A good man at one of these retreats had held a grudge against his community because he was convinced that his first wife had been discriminated against at the local hospital. She died and left him with a broken heart. His business flourished in that community and he became very wealthy. He remarried and it appeared he had a good life. But his anger toward those he suspected of religious discrimination had grown for over twenty years and sunk its roots deep in his soul. Those he accused of letting his wife die by refusing prompt treatment had long since retired or died. There was no one left to blame, yet his anger prevented progress in his love for God or people. During the course of the weekend, he surrendered his deep hurt to God and publicly declared his forgiveness of all those he blamed over the many years. He was wonderfully liberated and spent his remaining lifetime as a man in love with God and merciful toward people. He was a new man because he experienced renewal in his soul. When he forgave, the bitter root was extracted and the grace of God was able to reshape his soul.

Forgiving others is a prerequisite to spiritual renewal. The good news is that no matter how long the bitter roots of unforgiveness have been growing, the grace of God can transform us into the people God intended. God's grace works more quickly in positive transformation than can bitterness in hardening the heart. The gateway to the renewing grace of God is forgiving others.

A HUMAN NEED SINCE THE BEGINNING

Forgiving others is a human need. Humanity is better off forgiving than litigating. People are blessed by forgiving and cursed by revenge. Since we were created in the image of God, we need to forgive others to live up to that created human potential. Unfortunately, the story of the fall of man degrades into a story of blaming one another. Adam blamed both God and Eve ("The woman you put here with me—she gave me some fruit from the tree, and I ate it" (Genesis 3:12, NIV), and Eve faulted the snake ("Then the LORD God said to the woman, 'What is this you have done?' The woman said,

27

'The serpent deceived me, and I ate' (vs. 13). Soon revenge entered the human story by Cain and Abel, and the first murder occurred. Ever since then, the image of God appeared hidden by human behavior.

If blame had only been replaced by confession and absolution, how different history might have been. Failure to forgive will cause the inhumanity of Cain's revenge against Abel to become a pattern for our life even today. Such merciless apathy about another will rob us of the blessings for which we long. Mercy toward others restores the four blessings each one needs: regrets avoided, release of stress, response control, and spiritual renewal.

4

The Human Problem with Forgiving

"FORGIVE AND FORGET" are the most glibly spoken words in the human language. By the same token, the harsh words "I'll forgive but I'll never forget" are hardly worth the breath it takes to verbalize them. Forget? No human being is capable of forgetting nor does a single scripture require us to forget.

God repeatedly commands people to forgive and do so unconditionally. But God never asks us to forget, for that is a human impossibility. Memories are not choices. The only choice we have is whether to disarm our recollections through forgiveness. We cannot eliminate memories.

To Forget Is Divine

God alone is capable of forgiving and forgetting. God promises, "Their sins and lawless acts I will remember no more" (Hebrews 10:17).[26] Only God's nature is capable of eliminating memories. Human forgiveness does not mean the elimination of a memory, but the removal of blame. In our salvation, God both transfers the blame that belongs to us onto a sacrificial substitute and also eliminates the memory. But, to both remove the blame (forgive) and eliminate the memory (forget) is never a demand placed on people.

The human mind's capability is designed for information storage. We need to store information gained by experience in order to survive in life, and that process is known as learning. Once information about an experience is stored, it is also ready for retrieval. Retrieval is an active process subject to the will of the person and conditioned by one's mental aptitude.

However, storage of information is a passive process and occurs automatically. We routinely store emotional experiences, information about ourselves learned through social interaction, academic facts, and even hurtful experiences from the offenses of others against us. All of this is stored away and remains in the active files of our mind. Stored memories of hurts can unintentionally grow worse than the initial offense and remain active far longer than they are worth.

Suppressing Is not Forgetting

An attempt to forget about a hurt, instead of resolving to forgive it, is a temptation that we all face. We sometimes advise each other, "Oh, just forget about the hurt." We cannot just forget about it. We can only store it away in a file that will always be active.

In fact, when we attempt to forget and neglect to forgive, we succeed only in suppressing the memory. Some psychologists argue that it is possible to store negative traumatic memories in a file outside of the conscious mind. That file would be labeled "repressed memories."[27] These affect behavior in ways that appear irrational and inexplicable but actually are caused by such traumatic events that the memories have been pushed aside in order to survive them. Repressed memories are not the same as suppressed memories, which are far more common. Suppressed memories are unresolved issues which require only a reminder, not a repeat, to resurrect the initial emotional hurt.

During my junior high school years there was one student who worked hard at his tough guy, gang-leader image. This identity was fostered by his successful ploys of intimidation. He made threats just to enjoy any sign of fear from students who merely wanted to peaceably survive the school day. He worked as hard at intimidation as I did at showing no fear, but I secretly hoped my courage would never be tested.

Over twenty-five years after those tumultuous, hormonally imbalanced, early-adolescent years, I was visiting my hometown and heard his name announced over the public address system in a large facility. Though there was no visual contact, my body instinctively winced at the reminder of the person by the mere mention of his name. The secret fear had remained intact. Though I hadn't thought of him in nearly three decades, the involuntary defense reaction was still in place because I had only suppressed the memory. I had never released the person from the fear of him that I once harbored.

Even though the remembrances of these types of offenses are filed away in a seemingly distant place of our memory, they are amazingly accessible. Only a name needs to be spoken and our nerves react defensively. Perhaps it's not a name we hear but we encounter someone who benignly reminds us of the person who caused a hurt. The emotions will rush in and grip us with fear and defensiveness. Our suppressed memories cause us to victimize people who are guilty of nothing but reminding us of a person who once hurt us. Forgetting an offense doesn't resolve it because forgetting amounts to nothing more than merely suppressing.

A suppressed memory is always accessible and a full review of the painful incident is easily triggered. Our mind quickly locates that file, recollects the episode, and alerts a defense system of impending danger even when no real threat is present. We can have unexplained anger erupting at times that calmness and respect are needed. There could be no single reason for disliking an individual, but a similarity in personality triggers a search and review of a bad experience suppressed deep in our memory's file system. That memory is unresolved and fully armed because it was only suppressed and was never disarmed. Suppression does not disarm the memory; only forgiveness does.

DISARMING THE MEMORY

Forgiveness has the power to disarm the hurtful memory because it removes the need to blame. Without forgiveness, blame always seeks a new object upon which to attach itself. Then what happens is the one who is unaware receives the blame due someone else. Blame must find a target, for its nature is to pin the fault on someone. Putting something out of our mind does not remove the blame but merely suppresses it until a later time. Forgiving alone removes the need to blame even when we are reminded of the offense. Separating the offender from his or her sin removes the sting of hurt from the memory against which we are retaliating with blame and revenge. Forgetting is not a human possibility and suppression poses a problem when we confuse it with forgiveness. In fact, Archbishop Desmond Tutu has said, "Without memory there can be no healing,"[28] for without awareness of the event, the offended and offender are not able to reconcile. Removal of blame is needed rather than mere denial.

Forgiveness is not forgetting; it is a different way of remembering a person. Once the blame is removed, the memory may be redeemed for healing and ministry to others. One day someone reminded Clara Barton, founder of the American Red Cross, of a vicious deed that another person had done to her years before. Surprisingly, she acted as if she had never even heard of the incident.

"Don't you remember it?" her friend asked.

"No," said Barton. "I distinctly remember forgetting it."[29]

This was a play on words to let her friend know of the human impossibility of forgetting absolutely. Another memory had now been associated with the offense. Ms. Barton forgave the hurtful experience and found a different way of remembering it, one that removed the blame and redeemed both the forgiven and forgiver.

5

The Natural Problem
of Grudges

THE HUMAN CAPACITY for information storage not only prevents us from forgetting an offense, it also enables us to nurse our hurts. Grudge-bearing is the purposeful nourishing of a hurtful memory by rehearsing it. Suppressing a memory is very different because it is an attempt to put the painful memory to sleep, even though reminders keep waking it up. By contrast, grudge-bearing occurs when we nurse a hurt by willfully replaying the offense and planning our revenge. Because we cannot truly eliminate the memory of a cruel offense, we will be tempted to intentionally foster that memory by replaying it and justifying the anger that accompanies it.

NURSING THE GRUDGE

We have a natural tendency to give attention to our pain. When I endured several months of pain from a bulging disk in lumbar number five, I constantly nursed my ache. I talked about my experience and thought about the incidents that brought about my soreness. That was natural. More than once, my wife told me, "Stop talking about it so much." I really didn't realize how much the pain dominated my conversation.

In my case of the bulging disc, the appropriate nursing of the painful problem helped heal it. I applied cold packs. Had I applied heat to the already inflamed disc, the warmth may have felt soothing but would have furthered the inflammation. Heat was inappropriate nursing; ice was needed. Likewise, inappropriate attention to an emotional hurt inflames it.

Nursing a hurtful memory by replaying the offense and scheming about how to even the score is like applying heat to a condition requiring ice. The willful recollection of an offense is unsuitable because forgiveness is needed. Grudge-bearing has a strange way of making us feel strong when really it weakens us. That false strength seems to assuage the wound of victimization. Grudge-bearing creates a more volatile condition and increases the probability for an explosion. Because rehearsing the hurt and scheming someone's demise keeps the pain tender, some people exhibit abrupt anger whenever the conversation topic nears the matter of their previous wound. An outburst followed by angry words of justification as untrue as "I don't care what they think because that's just how I feel about it!" erupts even though no one was trying to argue.

Examples of this phenomenon are everywhere. For example, the dialogue in an office may simply mention how tensions at work can cause misunderstandings between office personnel. This will inflame the employee who is the scapegoat for the whole department's failure to perform, rendering him incapable of simple conversation about office relationships. Or only a mention about the game of basketball might cause an unexpected angry reaction from the media-maligned coach of this year's underachieving, mediocre team.

In these and other cases like them, one's defense mechanisms are initiated at the appearance of more potential criticism, though none was actually imminent. When we intentionally recall being the brunt of unfair blame or criticism, an emotional outburst is often caused by the painful memory that has been nursed along to an inflamed emotional state. Through grudge-bearing, the sensitive spot in our soul becomes worse than the affliction of the original offense.

Grudge-bearing remains a temptation even for the person who intends to forgive. The devil himself is intent upon undermining our best intention to pardon others. We can make a decision to forgive an offense and immediately we are presented with the temptation to rehearse the event that wounded us. At that point we will either reaffirm our forgiveness or recollect our hurt. Whichever we rehearse will determine our emotional and spiritual future. The human capacity to store information makes grudge-bearing a present possibility throughout our life. We have a choice and can refuse the temptation to nurse the hurt and rehearse the offense.

A Waste of Life

Grudge-bearing can waste our time and ultimately our life. Negative emotions prevent us from enjoying life's positive experiences. Bitterness robs us of joys. Bitterness destroys and doesn't achieve progress in any manner. It wastes our days and years and never contributes anything to them. Whenever I hear of a surviving family member pledging the remainder of his or her life to avenge a loved one's death, I always cringe. Now, two lives are wasted; one by murder and the other by grudge-bearing. It is strange that the pledge to bear the grudge actually makes the survivor feel strong in the face of the powerlessness of victimization. In truth, carrying that grudge squanders one's life and weakens the soul.

We have a choice about what will consume our lives. Gordon Wilson faced such a choice in 1987. He and his daughter, Marie, were victims of a bombing by the Provisional IRA during Ireland's religious civil war. She was twenty years old and a nurse. Marie's last words to her father were spoken on November 8, 1987, from underneath the rubble of the Poppy Day Bombing's aftermath. She said, "Daddy, I love you very much."

Wilson recounts, "Those were the last words she spoke to me. She still held my hand quite firmly and I kept shouting at her, 'Marie, are you all right?' but there wasn't a reply. We were there about five minutes. Someone came and pulled me out. I said, 'I'm all right but for God's sake my daughter is lying right beside me and I don't think she is too well.'"

Wilson was right. Marie didn't survive much longer. He goes on to talk about that incident. "She's dead. She didn't die there. She died later. The hospital was magnificent, truly impressive, and our friends have been great, but I miss my daughter, and we shall miss her but I bear no ill will, I bear no grudge."[30]

Gordon Wilson made a choice that he would spend his lifetime honoring his daughter and focusing on his faith instead of bearing a grudge. After his release from the hospital, Gordon Wilson led a crusade for Protestant-Catholic reconciliation. Protestant extremists who had planned to avenge the bombing decided that such behavior would be politically foolish because of the publicity surrounding Wilson. Wilson wrote a book about his daughter, spoke out against violence, and constantly repeated the refrain, "Love is the bottom line." He met with the IRA, personally forgave them for what they had done, and asked them to lay down their arms. "I know that you've lost loved ones, just like me," he told them. "Surely, enough is enough. Enough blood has been spilled." [31]

GRUDGE MAKES IMPACT

We can spend our lives collecting grudges as though we are stockpiling ammunition. People we do not intend to destroy will innocently step into the line of fire. There will inevitably be unintended casualties of our amassed anger. When we keep hurts simmering, we will be sensitive to the slightest irritation. A single reminder of any of those hurts, with which we were once inflicted, detonates the ammunition we stockpile.

Grudges are past hurts infected with bitterness. An inflamed personal injury will require more grace and more time to heal than the original offense. Without the act of forgiveness, a grudge may scab over but never heal because only forgiveness will cleanse the bitterness from the wound.

Even though our ability to store information makes grudge-bearing a natural possibility, we do not have to be victims. We are responsible for refusing to bear a grudge even if we feel it is very genuinely justified. Many natural impulses exist that make socially irresponsible behaviors real possibilities. Extramarital sexual urges are naturally felt but that is no excuse for acting them out. God and government demand that such impulses do not rule our lives. So grudge-bearing is a natural urge and is always possible, but forgiveness makes the refusal to bear a grudge equally possible. The choice is ours. One choice is wrong and is called sin. The other choice is healthy and right, and is called holiness and love.

Grudges can seem absurd to an objective listener. One community volunteer and responsible mother of a middle school student recalled an incident when her son was in the first grade. He was taunted and mistreated on the playground by another boy his age. She recounted this event to me six years after it had happened and was still visibly agitated. She volunteered, "I know that I shouldn't feel this way but I hate that..." and then named the boy who once had jeered at her son. Unless that mother learns how to forgive, she will still experience the full force of her anger at the sight of that boy walking the high school graduation line with her son. She had stored and rehearsed the incident; retained the associated anger; and allowed a long-lasting hatred to grow. If we hold onto a grudge, that grudge will hold onto to us and won't let go even after the grudge becomes rationally inexplicable.

Osama Bin Laden will go down in Western history as the most infamous of all grudge-bearers. Citing wrongdoings by Christians, some of which are over a millennium old, he achieved revenge on September 11, 2001. He is proof that grudge-bearing is a bequeathed commodity. Confusing a nation that accommodates Christianity with a nation that is authentically Christian in orientation, he expressed an ancient grudge by murdering over 3,000 innocent people. His only justification was that innocent lives from his nation have also been murdered. Bin Laden exemplified the words of the psalmist, "When my heart was grieved and my spirit embittered, I was senseless and ignorant; I was a brute beast before you" (Psalm 73:21-22). The reality is that his actions were morally depraved and strategically foolish. Grudges really are ludicrous even when they are religious.

No matter how naturally grudges emerge, we are still accountable when we nurse them. People have a free will and are accountable for choices, even difficult ones. Choices need to be motivated by the big picture of our responsibility to God and the result of our decisions. One day, the grudge-bearer will find out that the chip on his or her shoulder has the stronger grip. A well-stated line in the movie *Spiderman 3* summarizes the result of grudge-bearing: "Revenge in our heart… it can take you over. Before you know it, it can turn you into something ugly."[32]

6

The Divine Possibility
of Forgiveness

FORGIVENESS IS NOT an innate human capability but a divine possibility. The human experience does not have to be subject to endless grudge-bearing and revenge-seeking. Jesus came to invite us into the life made possible by God alone. Jesus invites us into the divine prospect of forgiving each other.

WHO CAN FORGIVE, BUT GOD ALONE

The Gospel about Jesus Christ teaches us that only God is able to forgive sin. In Luke chapter 5, we are told that Jesus was teaching in a crowded house in Capernaum, his home. A great crowd gathered at the house in which he would spend the evening. They surely came because they wanted to hear the adventure stories of Jesus' exciting ministry. After all, Jesus' popularity had swelled, and on that night even the doorway of the house was packed with people. He preached the good news to his hometown community on that night, just as he did so often elsewhere. News of this gathering spread quickly and others in the town heard about Jesus' visit.

Four men quickly conceived an idea concerning a paralytic friend of theirs. The paraplegic was blessed to have four friends so devoted to him. They seized the possibility of a divine, miraculous healing from Jesus and proved to be men of action. They would not be denied the cure if it at all depended upon them.

By the time they carried their friend to the house, the entrance was obstructed by the mass of people. Four men and a stretcher would never slip through that crowd. But these indomitable men did not waver. They carried their friend up to the roof and dug a hole through the thatches. Then they lowered the stretcher right in front of Jesus. They didn't need to verbalize their request because their action witnessed to their faith. Jesus certainly observed belief in action even if others regarded it as an intrusion.

Jesus' response wasn't what the crowd expected. Scripture gives no indication of any physical examination or verbal investigation. We know only that Jesus spoke directly to the man and his situation: "Friend, your sins are forgiven" (Luke 5:20). The paralytic's physical body was damaged, and the preacher speaks of spiritual healing? Could that make sense to the four friends or to us?

Jesus took that opportunity to reveal His divine identity. As soon as He spoke those words of forgiveness, the religious teachers in the crowd found fault. They kept their objections to themselves but knew that claiming to do what only God can do amounted to blasphemy. "Who can forgive sins but God alone?" they questioned (verse 21). They knew that no mere human being had the right or the capability to offer absolute forgiveness to another like Jesus just had to the paralytic. Only God can pronounce a person absolutely forgiven and to claim that authority was blasphemous.

Jesus knew their thoughts and we would assume that He might correct their thinking. This occasion could have been used as a teaching moment to explain how forgiving is everyone's potential. Surprisingly, Jesus affirmed their theological understanding. The religious teachers thought Jesus was equating Himself with God by making His statement of absolute forgiveness. He didn't correct their conclusion. Instead, Jesus proved that they were right by saying something else that only God has the authority to pronounce: "I tell you, get up, take your mat and go home" (verse 24).

Only God can instantaneously heal a paralytic and only God can forgive sins. Jesus revealed Himself as equal to God. The point of this teaching moment was to manifest the true identity of Jesus to us: He is the God who forgives us, just as He is the God who heals us. This occasion affirmed that forgiveness and miraculous healing are divine possibilities, not human capabilities.

THE GOOD NEWS OF DIVINE POSSIBILITY

The good news of Jesus is that He calls us into a life of divine possibilities. The invitation to discipleship is an invitation to live a life that only God can make possible. The church still experiences divine healing as a sign that God includes us in His kingdom now.[33] God's kingdom incorporates the experience of God's grace to forgive others because it is divinely possible. What is not humanly possible in the natural order of life is divinely possible in the kingdom of God, which we enter when we are born again (John 3:3). Therefore, forgiving each other is mandated because it has become possible for the born-again believer. This is a vitally important principle: since it is possible in Christ, forgiving others is commanded for Christians.

Forgiveness is always God's work in and through us. The command to forgive is intended to make us dependent upon what only God can do. We find ourselves utterly reliant upon God growing that forgiveness in us and saving us from a life of endless grudge-bearing. We can never claim to become a competent forgiver because the competence always belongs to God alone. Forgiving each other, much like ministry itself, is dependent upon God's achievement. "Not that we are competent in ourselves to claim anything for ourselves, but our competence comes from God. He has made us competent as ministers of a new covenant..." (2 Corinthians 3:5-6a).

Since forgiveness is God's activity and achievement in and through us, we must stop condemning ourselves for finding forgiveness humanly hard. Forgiving others is not difficult; it is humanly impossible. "Who can forgive sins but God alone?" (See Mark 2:7.) When we depend on our own resolve and resourcefulness in forgiving another, we will always be frustrated by that demand. The perceived difficulty of forgiving others is intended to drive us to a greater reliance on the work of the Holy Spirit. Forgiveness will always prove to be the achievement of God.

GOD GROWS THINGS

Anything God accomplishes in us after new birth in Christ is grown in us. The fruit of the Spirit illustrates that well. The production of the sanctifying work of the Spirit is wonderfully summarized by the qualities of love, joy, peace, patience, kindness, goodness, faithfulness, gentleness, and self-control (Galatians 5: 22-23). These qualities of Christ's character are fruit and they are grown, not manufactured. Growing in the grace and knowledge of our Lord and Savior Jesus Christ really means that God's achievement (grace) produces characteristics in growing measure (2 Peter 3:18). While we must take responsibility for our lives and yield our choices fully to God's will, the produce of God's grace is grown in time. The Lord Jesus taught this same truth in the parable of the vine and the branches (John 15: 1-8).

Everything that grows does so in stages. A fruit-bearing tree displays stages of growth every season. There are twenty-seven stages of growth in the fruit of the apple or pear tree before the harvest.[34] Identifying the stages of growth assures the farmer that all is well with the tree prior to the production of mature fruit. The harvest is assured because the stages of growth are recognized. As long as the farmer observes the progression of sequential stages, he is satisfied by the legitimate anticipation of a good harvest.

God grows forgiveness for others in the soil of our souls as we yield our will to the Father and to the resources of the Holy Spirit. Forgiveness is also grown in observable stages. In the early stages of the growth we may struggle with forgiveness and even question whether we have forgiven at all. It is easy to become discouraged as we forgive each other when old feelings of hurt and anger invade the peace we thought our soul possessed. In that moment we are tempted with despair. We may wonder if God even heard our prayer for grace to forgive.

Stages of Growth

The truth is that God is indeed producing forgiveness but we might fail to recognize its stages of growth. If we can identify those stages, we would be able to live in anticipatory joy, even while we struggle in the process. The joy comes from observing God growing forgiveness even while we wait for the harvest of maturity. We may be tempted with grudges but our hope is affirmed by observing the progress. The stages of forgiveness enable us to confess that God *is* growing it in us. We are not required to watch carefully for each stage, but observation of the stages will assure us of the Spirit's movement in our soul.

Six Stages of Forgiving Others

The stages of growth in forgiveness may follow one another quite simply and easily. On the other hand, each stage may prove to be difficult and growth may be a struggle. In either case, the Christian may rest in the truth that God is working. The believer is called to wait on God as the fruit of a forgiving heart is grown. Though waiting may be a bit thorny, it is always a state in which we are surrounded by God's assurances. "Be still before the Lord and wait patiently for him" (Psalm 37:7b).

When a Christian fully submits to the leadership of the Holy Spirit and surrenders the hurt of an offense to Jesus, God begins growing forgiveness in the soul. However, forgiveness is not automatic nor does it grow without facing challenges. Within our humanity are obstacles to forgiveness. Our natural memory is an obstacle, as is the temptation to repeatedly replay the offense. These obstacles oppose any success at forgiveness and incline us toward grudge-bearing.

Our hope is Jesus' invitation to the life that God alone makes possible. In Christ, natural obstacles to forgiveness are no longer limitations and can be overcome. Life in God's kingdom is a participation in God's forgiving character. "Through these he has given us his very great and precious promises, so that through them you may participate in the divine nature" (2 Peter 1:4). Through God's nature at work in us, forgiveness grows, like the fruit of the Spirit, and does so in observable stages. Ensuing chapters will identify six stages of forgiveness. When God achieves any one of these stages, we have reason to trust God for the full maturity of forgiveness.

SECTION TWO

HOW FORGIVENESS WORKS

7

The First Stage of Forgiveness: Willingness

Lord, make me willing to forgive.

THE FIRST STAGE of God's work of forgiveness is the willingness to grant it. In order to grow in God's grace for pardoning others, we must surrender the right to remain angry. Why do we even consider ourselves to have such a right? It is our sinful nature that feels strong when we are angry and we can become inebriated with that emotion. A person under the influence of alcohol may feel strong but is actually entirely dysfunctional. So it is with anger; it actually weakens our ability to respond productively and act wisely in life. Graciously, God answers our cry for help in forgiving others by leading us in surrendering our right to remain angry.

We deceive ourselves if we bypass this very important stage of growth in forgiving others. The truth is that after I am hurt by another's offense, I am *not* willing to forgive. Most likely, I am only willing to get even after being hurt.

The person who does not acknowledge the genuine desire of the heart for revenge in the aftermath of a hurt often lives in a state of denial. Pretending never allows us to progress toward genuine forgiveness because it actually prevents stage one, which is the willingness to forgive. Granting forgiveness requires a movement of our will in the opposite direction from harboring anger. Our will cannot move toward two opposing goals simultaneously.

SURRENDERING

Forgiveness begins when a person abandons revenge entirely and surrenders all rights to it. The will of a person must yield this right to the will of God who then leads us into the possibilities of His nature. Upon abandonment of revenge and surrender to God's plan for us, the Holy Spirit then begins to grow forgiveness. We begin to observe God's work in our soul when we recognize that we have become willing to forgive.

When God grows something in us, He begins with our desires. "Delight yourself in the Lord and he will give you the desires of your heart" (Psalm 37:4). What does God give? God gives the desire that is fitting for a person who delights in the Lord. The whole life of a disciple of Christ begins with a genuine transformation of our desire. While the disciple denies himself, he does so because of a love for God more than for anything else in life. The desire for God becomes the chief motivator in the life of Jesus' followers. The pearl of great price is fellowship with God, and selling all that one has represents the subsequent act of denying oneself in this life in order to experience God forever (Matthew 13:44-46). The desire for something better was the first movement of the Spirit in our salvation and is also called conviction (John 16:8).

Genuine Desire

The Christian's life is not some alien experience, but an authentic human one that is possible only with God. No one lives a fruitful Christian life against his or her desires. God transforms our desire so that all of life in Christ is exactly what we genuinely want, "…for it is God who works in you *to will* and to act according to his good purpose" (Philippians 2:13, italics added). Therefore, forgiving others begins with this prayer: *Lord, make me willing to forgive.* This does not imply that conflicting desires won't also compete for our allegiance, but we cannot deny the real existence of the desire to forgive once God has grown it. Perhaps it is noticed right after a specific prayer time or when we least expect it but the words, "I want to forgive," come to mind. We may not yet be ready to act on the correct desire, as will be required in time, but certainly the desire has grown. God is at work.

The first stage of anything God does is a transformation of desire. Discipleship is not merely an external experience but it is an intrinsic one; there is a change in the inner person. So it is with forgiveness. God transforms our desire so that we really want to forgive. When God works, the Christian's response is not coerced and forgiveness is not forced. The moral demand of forgiving others becomes one's own desire and is then willingly offered.

When Unwillingness Is Deeply Ingrained

In stage one of growing in God's grace for forgiveness, we may find ourselves needing to pray several layers deep. *Lord, make me willing to be willing to forgive.* The truth is that we are sometimes so far removed from a willingness to forgive that we must pray about our unwillingness. Our desire to be angry may be so ingrained that we need to ask God to make us *want* to be willing. For example, the letter from our estranged spouse's lawyer demands an amount of money that cripples our future and we do not naturally respond with a willingness to forgive. We even fear that surrendering our right to remain angry might require that we have to live under an oppressive situation forever. That is not true. We may not be able to live with a situation, but forgiving others will prevent that situation from living in us. So we turn to God and by faith present our angry heart with repentance and ask God to crucify it with Christ because we are unable to slay that anger on our own. God will answer that prayer because He provided for it at the cross. "I have been crucified with Christ and I no longer live, but Christ lives in me. The life I live in the body, I live by faith in the Son of God, who loved me and gave himself for me" (Galatians 2:20).

Usually, when we lack a genuine willingness to forgive we are not yielded to God's will. The lack of obedience to God's mandate indicates that our life is influenced more by the worldliness of earthly life than the holiness of eternal life. Repentance is the solution to our lack of motivation. Many Christians have become frustrated with the whole of the Christian life because of some unforgiven offense about which they retain the right to remain angry. Even though they might be more than glad to teach Sunday school, serve in the church's kitchen, or sit on the church board, their enthusiasm for following Jesus ebbs away. Many would then tell us either to be more committed to Christ's work or take more time for rest and relaxation. Both of those options misdiagnose the problem and result in unwarranted guilt concerning our weak commitment or surprising apathy toward the church. The problem is an unwillingness to either confess a sin or forgive one.

In the early days of municipal power grids, a boy received an electric train set from a wealthy uncle for his birthday. He and his dad meticulously set up the track on a plywood base in the garage and placed the trains on the track with all the props around it. They plugged the set's transformer into the household outlet and hoped to watch the train chug around the model city. To their horror the opposite happened. The houselights extinguished. Furthermore, the streetlights shut off. The entire neighborhood lost its electrical power.

When the power company arrived to investigate, they found the short circuit in the home with the new train set. A three-inch nail lying across the track had caused a short in the unprotected wiring that was directly connected to the grid's local transformer. Only one small nail that lay haphazardly on the track stopped both the little train and the neighborhood's lights. Without the power, the train set only looked good, but it wasn't much fun to play with.

In the same way, only one intentionally unforgiven offense can derail the progress of anyone's growth in Christ and can prevent the power of the Holy Spirit from renewing our motivation to follow Jesus. No amount of church work or recreation and rest will compensate for what only repentance can do. When we repent, the willingness to forgive is restored and the Christian life again becomes a source of joy.

Once we relinquish all our resistance to becoming genuinely willing to forgive, then our prayer to become willing produces results. The Holy Spirit is impeded only by our unwillingness to yield our rights for vindication or for feeling victimized. When we begin to pray, "Lord make me willing," God works at loosening the grip of unyieldingness. The Spirit's activity may be accompanied by emotional turmoil for a divine plow is conditioning our soul for receptivity so mercy can grow. Once freed from our stubborn refusal, the Holy Spirit is unhampered in growing an authentic willingness to forgive.

NOTHING MAGICAL OR MANUFACTURED

The growth of a genuine willingness to forgive is not instantaneous. It must mature so that its roots dig deep in our soul. The readiness to forgive must become so ingrained in our desire that we are not later prone to change our mind. The Holy Spirit cultivates our willingness so well that we become highly motivated to appropriate all of God's grace to forgive a particular offense. Therefore, we continue to pray for willingness and wait on God to accomplish it. We remain yielded to God's authority in this matter, even while we're waiting to become genuinely agreeable to forgive. By remaining yielded, we won't squander time by justifying feelings of revenge.

Then one day, we wake up or are walking along and we realize that we are genuinely and thoroughly willing to forgive the person who hurt us. We may not be fully able to forgive yet, but we have become willing. God has grown stage one of forgiveness. We recognize that only God can produce such a willingness to forgive. The willingness to forgive will be as obvious as a blossom on a tree and we will detect a sincere desire to release the person who hurt us from the wrong he or she inflicted upon us. Even if a preexisting resistance challenges the new willingness, we will recognize that God has begun a new work in us that did not exist earlier.

When God is finished growing willingness, we will not begrudge forgiveness or feel coerced, but will authentically desire to release that person from their sin. The desire to forgive will be consistently present. Our willingness to forgive will overcome our temptation to pursue revenge because God has effected that willingness and is able to sustain it because the one who is in you is greater than the one who is in the world (1 John 4:4).

No Expected Time Frame

Whether willingness is grown in one's soul within an hour, a day, a week, or even a year is not the issue. As we mature in Christ, our soul becomes more receptive and prepared to assimilate God's work of grace. But the growth needed in our willingness to forgive the hurt of a bitter divorce may very well require a longer period of time than the willingness needed to forgive an insulting joke. Willingness to forgive a repeat offender may very well take more time to grow than a hurtful word spoken by an otherwise-loving spouse on one occasion. That time frame makes no difference in the grand scheme of life. God's grace is sufficient to grow the willingness to forgive in due time. The willingness to forgive will always be there on time when we are fully yielded to the Holy Spirit.

There is no need to play-act this stage of growth in God's grace for forgiving others. We can't progress past the stage God is presently growing. The Spirit has finished the first stage of willingness when we authentically and consistently want to forgive. Then, and only then, do we begin the next stage—the ability to forgive someone. We must not confuse *willingness* with *ability*. They are two separate achievements of God's grace, even if they happen to be accomplished simultaneously.

The willingness to forgive is the first stage of growth. We can take joy in the fact that God's grace is growing forgiveness within us. God has begun and "...he who began a good work in you will carry it on to completion until the day of Christ Jesus" (Philippians 1:6).

8

The Second Stage of Forgiveness: Ability

Lord, make me able to forgive.

THE WILLINGNESS TO forgive has grown in stage one. Now we face a new frontier because we want to forgive, but can we? It would be much easier (or at least more familiar) to suppress the hurt. It would be easier yet to nurse the hurt. We are fully aware of the possibility of failing to forgive and becoming consumed with anger all over again. If I forgive, can I make it last? Can I think about that person without dredging up the past hurt and feeling its sting again?

These are issues of ability. Removing the stinger from a hurtful memory is no small matter and we are afraid of failing to do so. However, the fear of failing in our intent to forgive is met by the assurance of God's grace. Only God can forgive. Only God's grace assures that the second stage of forgiveness will grow just like the first stage did.

We begin by asking God to make us able to forgive. We acknowledge our inability and the natural lack of fitness for the spiritual demand of forgiveness. In the face of the need to forgive, we recognize that we are weak "but the Spirit helps us in our weakness" (Romans 8:26). Recognizing our absolute need, and relying on God's absolute grace, enable the Holy Spirit to grow the ability to forgive another. Our role is to yield all our entitlements continuously, and to trust God to answer our prayer, *Lord, make me able to forgive.*

GOD'S ENABLING PROMISE

Will God grow the ability to forgive within us? Jesus answers that question in a parable about prayer. The answer, of course, is an unequivocal *Yes.*

> Which of you fathers, if your son asks for a fish, will give him a snake instead? Or if he asks for an egg, will give him a scorpion? If you then, though you are evil, know how to give good gifts to your children, how much more will your Father in heaven give the Holy Spirit to those who ask him.
>
> —Luke 11:11-13

God would love to give you the ability to forgive the person who hurt you. Pardoning others is God's command to us and, therefore, is unquestionably God's will for us. There is a promise concerning prayer requests, which are clearly aligned with God's desire for us. The promise says, "This is the confidence we have in approaching God: that if we ask anything according to his will, he hears us. And if we know that he hears us—whatever we ask—we know that we have what we asked of him" (1 John 5:11-13). God delights in His children coming in faith and dependence to obtain what only the Father can give.

The Second Stage of Forgiveness: Ability

The expectations of Christian discipleship place us in a position of faith and reliance upon God. In the kingdom of God, dependence upon the Holy Spirit is a normal condition of life. Our natural inability to forgive others will remind us that we really are dependent upon the Spirit. Forgiving others would be impossible otherwise. The ability to be unaffected by a previous hurt as we forgive and then relate graciously to the one we forgave will require continuous reliance upon God's grace. Apart from God's grace, anger and resentment will work their way back into our lives.

Forgiving others by God's grace is *receivable* rather than *achievable*. We must ask God, out of our hunger and thirst, to give us the ability to forgive. As Jesus said, "Blessed are those who hunger and thirst for righteousness, for they will be filled (Mathew 5:6). There is nothing casual or inconsequential about asking God for the ability to forgive. If the ability to forgive is a proposition for which we don't yearn, then we are not in a position to receive God's grace for it. We must then go back to the earlier prayer, "Lord make me *more* willing to forgive."

When we do ask God with a passionate desire, with a reliance on the Holy Spirit, and with faith in God's promise, then God will give us the ability to forgive. We must remain in a position of desire, reliance, and trust while we wait on God to grow the ability to forgive deep into our soul. Then one day, we will realize that we really can forgive and that God is cultivating that ability.

RECEPTIVITY AND TIME FRAME

As we grow into Christian maturity, we became more receptive and receive the divine ability to forgive more quickly. We also learn how to yield and remain yielded. We find out how to rely on God's ability more fully. We discover that we can trust God for greater challenges. And we even understand how to wait on God productively. Our maturation can be measured by how quickly we become able to forgive. Jesus was able to forgive even while He was being crucified.

A new believer may require months of exercising and grooming the soul before the ability to forgive is grown. The weeds of revenge and resentment are so deeply rooted because of our experience in the world that the Holy Spirit must work overtime to cultivate the soul for the first stage of willingness, usually by breaking our will and allowing our hearts to be broken as well. Then, the unfamiliarity of forgiveness might impede the soul's receptivity to God's grace growing the second stage of ability. Learning to surrender and rely will determine the time required for the growth of ability, but the Spirit always triumphs in the life of a yielded believer.

No Standard Time Frame

This stage of forgiveness, like all of the others, is simple and succinct but not necessarily quick. We should not confuse the brevity of the description with the speed of its delivery. The process of authentic forgiveness may require years. The time does not indicate the authenticity of God's grace working in us. When we are wronged in a way we have never before encountered, even the most seasoned Christian among us may experience only the proficiency of a novice in forgiving. Every one of us is, after all, a learner.

My daughter should have called me right away, but as a senior in high school, she was prone to treat casually those matters I treat critically and urgently. Imagine that! Late for school and changing lanes on the highway, she misjudged the speed of the vehicle that she had moved behind. Their bumpers connected but there was no significant impact, so this fact added to her casual regard for the minor accident. The police filed a report indicating correctly that it was my daughter's fault and the other driver was provided our insurance information. The point of contact left some of my daughter's car's paint and an impression noticeable only by careful inspection on her rear bumper on the right side.

Some days later I called the other driver and asked her to send the bill to me rather than the insurance company in order to keep my premiums lower. When the bill for over $400 came a few weeks later, I was shocked! I called to ask the other driver for a personal inspection and explanation for the work done. We agreed to meet at her home. My daughter and I arrived at the appointed time and walked through her living room to the garage. I noticed that it was a nicely appointed home, well beyond the means of a salary in her line of work. Living in her home were several disabled adults who were likely recipients of disability income. I naturally suspected that she was profiteering from disability money, and that bothered me.

She took us to her vehicle and my daughter identified it. She explained that a taillight, quarter panel, and even side panel were replaced because the collision had damaged them. Strangely, the bumper was still not repaired and the paint from my daughter's car was still visible! The slight impression on the bumper was the same as it had been the day of the accident.

When I asked why it hadn't been repaired, she explained that they hadn't "gotten to it yet." I was suspicious and told her so. She defended herself and said that she took the car directly to the car-body repair shop "from the scene of the accident, that very day." She claimed that in the judgment of the body-shop technician, the repair work was necessary as a result of that accident. I went home and looked at the repair bill again and discovered that she had lied about when she had taken the car to the shop. The invoice from the repair shop appeared entirely unrelated to the slight collision and reflected damage to the car from an earlier incident. I hate when people lie to me, and when it involves my daughter, I might even become somewhat assertive.

I couldn't afford that bill nor should I have paid it so I told the woman to submit it to my insurance company. Then I appealed directly to the insurance adjuster and let them know of the lie. The insurance company had "bigger fish to fry" and they just paid it. Underneath, I was seething. After another accident, the insurance company chose to drop us as clients. That result added to an emerging bitterness toward the woman. In our small town, we can't truly avoid one another. In order to overcome recurring feelings of bitterness, I began to pray about forgiveness. *Lord make me willing,* I silently prayed.

In time, I did become willing and I began to note that she works in a nursing home, taking care of people largely forgotten by society. I continued to pray, *Lord, make me able* (the next stage), and I began to rethink my conclusion about her profiteering from the disability income of those who lived in her home. I realized that she was taking care of them and they were well off in her home. One stage led to another, and even though almost two years passed by, I moved on to stages three and four in which I forgave her. The first three stages took the most time. This story will be continued in the chapters on the last of the stages.

Time is not as relevant as direction in the sanctifying work of the Spirit. Neither should time be a measure of the Spirit's enabling forgiveness. It is far more dangerous to speed through the stages of forgiveness spuriously. Forgiveness cannot be forced or faked, so we must allow the growth of forgiveness to take the time it needs. Please keep that in mind as you consider this stage of growth as well as the next ones.

Once a Christian recognizes that God's grace has grown the ability to forgive, the baton of responsibility is transferred from God's initiative to that of the yielded person. Now the task of forgiving others requires our decision and action. The next stage of forgiveness depends upon us.

9

The Third Stage of Forgiveness: Decision

Choose to Forgive

THERE IS NOTHING automatic about our experience of the Christian faith. Any work that God accomplishes in us must also be appropriated into our life by faith as an act of our will. Faith is a movement of our will in response to God's initiative, a choice to trust and then to act accordingly. God's work doesn't bypass our volition. God's grace works forgiveness for others into our soul but we can forfeit that work if we fail to act on it. God works it *in* and the Christian must work it *out* (Philippians 2:12).

DECISIVE LIVING

Forgiveness requires an act of the will. Stage three requires the Christian to commit to a particular course of action, trusting God to make it possible. The Christian must make a decision to forgive. The baton of responsibility is passed from God to the believer. In stages one and two, the believer waits on God to work. In stages three and four, God waits on us to respond. In stage three our response is volitional, and in stage four it is practical. In stage three the believer must choose to forgive.

A decision bridges a desire to an action. A couple may be in love, want to spend all their time together, discover that they are both suited for each other, and desire to spend their life together. Yet if the desire and suitability are not followed by a decision to marry, the relationship will sour and frustrate one or both partners. A decision must follow a desire, or the process that began with willingness and matured into ability will be aborted prematurely and needlessly. There are many Christians who desire to be more forgiving and gracious but don't do it. Many Christians have wished to forgive and overcome the grudge, but the truth is that such a wish requires a choice to forgive, a decision for which God waits. The forgiveness of others, for which we wish, is not automatic.

Following Jesus was not automatic even for the disciples in the New Testament. Jesus invited the twelve, but all needed to make the decision to follow. Jesus also tells of people who heard the call and wanted to delay their response. Or, they heard the call, began to respond, but didn't remain committed to that response.

> As they were walking along the road, a man said to him, "I will follow you wherever you go." Jesus replied, "Foxes have holes and birds of the air have nests, but the Son of Man has no place to lay his head." He said to another man, "Follow me." But the man replied, "Lord, first let me go and bury my father." Jesus said to him, "Let the dead bury their own dead, but you go and proclaim the kingdom of God." Still another

said, "I will follow you, Lord; but first let me go back and say good-by to my family." Jesus replied, "No one who puts his hand to the plow and looks back is fit for service in the kingdom of God."

—Luke 9:57-62

Decisiveness is necessary from the beginning and through-out the Christian experience.

The Cost of a Decision

A decision is the threshold many do not want to cross. A decision frightens us because it seems so final. The choice to follow Christ means to abandon worldliness. The pledge to marry someone means to abandon all other romantic possibilities "for as long as you both shall live." The price of any decision is the loss of other options. A decision to forgive means that we can never again hold that hurt against the other. "Never again" is a long time and we intuitively will analyze the cost of that resolve. We know that in forgiveness we surrender a weapon of blame with which we can never again punish that person by reminding them of, or repaying them for, the hurtful act. In the choice to forgive, we lay down the right to ever again call that person a jerk.

Decisions Determine Who We Become

Deciding to forgive is not a casual matter. Every decision we make impacts the course of our lives. A series of small bad choices is as destructive as one large one. Most of us are good decision-makers on the major, defining choices such as marriage and career. However, our lives can become frustrating and unsatisfying because of a long series of poor decisions, even though each of them seemed inconsequential at the time. In that vein, the many decisions to forgive or to withhold forgiveness will determine whether we become loving or cynical.

After years of blaming and grudge-bearing, a good friend and parishioner became a sarcastic personality and suspicious about anyone she did not know well. At the same time, she did not experience God's love as a personal reality. Her cynicism actually prevented her from becoming vulnerable toward God and perceiving His unfailing love. How she longed for the assurance of God's gracious acceptance and affection. In her case, a life in politics had fostered a contemptuous attitude. The partisan infighting in that business left all participants wary of one another. After leaving her politically-based job, she began to let go of her pessimism about everyone, and slowly grace began to transform her disposition and faith. As she is deciding to forgive, she also experiences God's grace more personally and reflects that change in her relationships.

To continue appropriating God's grace to grow forgiveness, we must make the decision to forgive. God's grace waits for each one of us. Our decision unlocks the access to the deepest part of our soul where the hurt resides. Once we make the decision to forgive, the Holy Spirit fills us with the resources necessary for becoming free from that grudge.

Make the decision to forgive. God will enable us to make that resolve succeed. We are on our way to being free. The choice to show mercy is the threshold to God's power for forgiving people who hurt us.

10

The Fourth Stage of Forgiveness: Action

A DEFINITE ACTION MUST follow a decision. If a decision of any kind fails to result in a definite action, then the decision becomes void. A decision to marry someone must result in a definite wedding date. A resolve to attend college must follow with submitting an application. A choice to forgive someone must be followed by a definite act of forgiveness. Without a specific action, a decision to forgive becomes null and void with the passage of time.

A TANGIBLE ACTION

Every step of progress in the Christian's life rests on action points. The decision to live as a Christian is initiated by an act of conversion, which involves the mind, spirit and body. In many church traditions, that action point is a physical kneeling at an altar of prayer or a walk down the aisle in response to the invitation to come forward. Most every church tradition marks the act of conversion by a physical, water baptism. That definite act of baptism is a biblical expression of the decision to become a Christian.

The fourth stage, which is a definite act of forgiveness, must be tangible enough to mark the moment of decision in stage three. The purpose of baptism is to mark the fact of our conversion and it helps us in times of self-doubt or spiritual uncertainty. A clear resolve to forgive must be tangible enough to mark the event of forgiving someone. There will come times of doubt when old feelings of a grudge pass through our mind. There will be times of spiritual doubt about our choice to forgive when the same person repeats the same hurtful offense. If we do not make a definite act of forgiveness, we will be tempted to think that we failed to forgive. In reality, we did forgive but failed to make it tangible enough to overcome doubt.

A tangible act of forgiveness can fall into two categories and they merit examination: *inter*personal or a mutually experienced reconciliation and *intra*personal or a one-sided decision to forgive.

A FACE-TO-FACE RECONCILIATION

The treasurer of our church was a seasoned Christian. He was in retirement and used his free time to serve the Lord. He was a genuine Christian, but for some time had been irritated by another older man in our church. The other man was also a seasoned Christian, but he had an irritating habit of interrupting other people's conversations in order to speak. He would actually turn his back to one person in order to hijack the conversation already in progress. It was rude but not motivated by malice; it was insensitive and thoughtless but not mean-spirited. The treasurer felt like he had seen that good brother's backside one too many times. A hurt was registered and began to become infected with bitterness.

The Fourth Stage of Forgiveness: Action

Sometime later, I was serving communion during a regular worship service of our church. As we distributed the communion elements and asked people to wait to partake in order to prepare their hearts, the Holy Spirit began to work in the treasurer's soul. He could not take communion as long as he harbored this grudge. I noticed his nonparticipation because he sat about nine feet from where I stood. A pastor comes to know the worship habits of his people and it seemed very unusual for him to refrain from communion.

After that service I saw two older men in the lobby of our church, namely the two Christian brothers I have described. They were engaged in a conversation and concluded it with a brotherly handshake and embrace. One person forgave the other. It was a definite act that became a blessing for both. The treasurer was released from a grudge. The other man became willing to learn courtesy. Both good, spirit-filled Christian men experienced God's grace of forgiveness in a way that left no doubt because it was a definite act of mutual reconciliation. Subsequently, both men met with me and shared this testimony.

A PERSONAL BUT NOT MUTUALLY TRANSACTED FORGIVENESS

In most cases, the person who hurt us is either not aware of, or will not acknowledge, any fault. This is common. Forgiving a person who does not recognize a fault or desire to be pardoned is still a demand of holiness. Forgiveness initiates reconciliation more often than does apology.

Jesus initiated God's forgiveness while we were still sinning against Him. "But God demonstrates his own love for us in this: While we were still sinners, Christ died for us" (Romans 5:8). God's forgiveness initiates; admitting to the offense and receiving the forgiveness is our response. A one-sided transaction of forgiveness is an act of faith in God's ability to achieve it independently of a response or even an admission. A personal but unilaterally transacted forgiveness must be particularly definite in order to survive the nagging doubt that generally follows. We must be able to remember the act of forgiving another and we need a tangible mark of that moment of forgiveness. The less mutual the transaction of forgiveness, the more tangible it must be.

When we initiate forgiveness without the other person's participation, we benefit most often from a written act of forgiveness. Writing is a tangible and definite act. The piece of paper on which we write should not be sent or viewed by another. It may be saved for a while or shredded along with the stinger that our forgiveness has removed from the memory of the offense and reminder of the person. That piece of paper must never, under any circumstances, be used as a weapon of relational conflict! However, that written transaction of forgiveness becomes a spiritual benefit when we find it in our drawer or purse weeks or months afterward. It reminds us of the spiritual victory and assures us that God continues to grow forgiveness in stages five and six.

When we write out our forgiveness, we must be definite about what, who, and when we forgive. We must write something similar to the following:

*I forgive*_____ *for* _____
                [name]   [offense]

this day, _____.
              [date]

_____
              [Your Signature]

As we write, we must transfer our trust from our inability to forgive to God's ability to produce forgiveness in us. This transfer is not so much a writing exercise as it is a spiritual one. We are forgiving someone by a definite act of faith, and by writing we make it tangibly verifiable.

As we practice forgiveness over a period of years, the writing can be replaced by verbalization. An experienced forgiver can speak the words of forgiveness in prayer as a definite act of forgiving the offender. Verbalizing is also tangible even if it isn't as retrievable as a written declaration. Still, a verbal act of faith at a distinct point in time is enough to save a soul from hell; it can also be enough to remove the stinger of hurt from a wrongdoing.

AN ACT OF FORGIVENESS IS ALWAYS AN ACT OF FAITH

In making a definite act of forgiveness, we begin a course of action that only God is able to accomplish. This is like the wedding day which follows the decision of engagement and begins a new life. Following that definite act may come times when we feel committed to an impossible obligation. But, we learn to rest more fully on God's grace: "…for it is God who works in you to will and to act according to his good purpose" (Philippians 2:13). In stages one, two, and three, we see God's hand working in our volition. In stages four, five, and six, we experience God's hand enabling us to act on His command to forgive.

11

The Fifth Stage of Forgiveness: Overcoming

Confess the truth in the face of doubt.

FEELINGS LINGER LONG after their validity has expired. It is quite normal for old feelings of grudge to persist some time after forgiveness has been transacted. Even though one has forgiven, the painful feelings associated with the pardoned grudge keep hanging around. Those feelings *can* be overcome.

A PLACE FOR FEELINGS

We need to understand the role of feelings in the Christian's life. First, feelings are designed to follow obedience or disobedience. Feelings of joy or peace follow acts of obedient faith. Sometimes those feelings of joy follow at some distance behind obedience but they do not fail to arrive. Feelings are not designed to lead our faith. Many people wait for a feeling to inspire them to obedience but live in spiritual defeat, for feelings do not lead well. Some even follow the feelings produced by temptation into sin thinking that if it feels good, it is God's leading. Eventually disobedience gives way to the sinking feeling of regret—a secret emotion that most everyone has known.

Faith must lead a Christian's actions, and feelings should only follow. A feeling of peace that surpasses understanding follows a faith-led act of prayer with thanksgiving (Philippians 4:6-7). Generally, we don't pray because of feelings of peace. Instead, we pray because we lack peace. We turn to our faith, which leads us to prayer and then the peace follows.

Second, feelings are not designed to transmit truth. Faith alone is equipped to tell us what is true. Feelings cannot convey the truth consistently and should not be trusted to do so. When we think about all the times we did act on feelings, we recognize that those acts led us to regrettable decisions. Even if a hunch is a valid way to act on a business opportunity, it will not guide to what is true from God's perspective. Even the feeling of a clear conscience does not indicate whether we are innocent or guilty. "My conscience is clear, but that does not make me innocent. It is the Lord who judges me" (1 Corinthians 4:4). Paul did not even rely on the feeling of a clear conscience to tell him the truth about himself. He turned to the objectivity of God's Word.

Third, feelings need to be informed and corrected from within our soul. Our faith must correct our feelings, not the other way around. King David demonstrates how his faith corrected his feelings in Psalm 42. In that psalm, David articulates his feeling of depression.

My tears have been my food day and night, while men say to me all day long, "Where is your God?" These things I remember as I pour out my soul: how I used to go with the multitude, leading the procession to the house of God, with shouts of joy and thanksgiving among the festive throng.

—Psalm 42:3-4

Then, David's faith calls his feelings into question: "Why are you downcast, O my soul? Why so disturbed within me?" (42:5a). The victorious Christian experience is not without errant feelings. However, the victorious Christian calls into question the validity of those feelings in light of the Christian faith, which is entirely formed by the Word of God. We need to be led by that faith which beckons people to God and calls one to a point of conversion. That faith is objective and apostolic, because it is subject to the Bible rather than to our feelings.

Our feelings are unable to tell us the truth. Our feelings have told us that sin is okay, lust is healthy, argumentativeness is productive, and slander is simply a matter of being honest. If we only feel it, we ought not to trust it; we should test it by God's Word. Faith in God is not a fleeting feeling but a step of obedience to God's word and will.

Let's look at David's psalm again. After his faith calls his feelings into question, David corrects his feeling by what his faith informs him is true: "Put your hope in God, for I will yet praise him, my Savior and my God" (42:5b-6a). Such a corrective conversation between our faith and feelings is the normal course of the victorious Christian life. Faith leads, feelings follow; they should never be confused for one another.

Faith and Feelings of Grudge

Old feelings of grudge must also be informed of the truth and corrected by our faith. We really did forgive and are trusting God for the Spirit's work in our soul. God really did promise to work in us "to will and to act according to His good purpose."[35] We acted on God's promise and tangibly forgave the other person by faith. Old feelings of grudge are simply errant ones. As feelings often are, they are out of alignment with the truth, which is why our faith must inform our soul and correct errant feelings.

OVERCOME FEELINGS OF GRUDGE BY CONFESSING FAITH

After the act of forgiveness, lingering feelings of a grudge are corrected by a positive confession. The offense was forgiven and we know that forgiveness was transacted in good faith. We know it because we were present at that transaction. God's promises were relied upon and the act of forgiveness was carried out. Now, our feelings of grudge must be brought into alignment with the truth. We must confess the truth about our forgiveness. As often as we might experience the feelings of grudge, we must answer it with a confession of our forgiveness.

Confessing the truth strengthens our faith. We recite creeds because our confession of the truth strengthens our objective beliefs in the face of life's confusion. We remember and recall our moment of conversion to strengthen our subjective and personal experience of faith in the face of self-doubt. Our verbal recitation of creeds and our recollection of our conversion experience are ways of recalling our identity with Christ in the face of feelings that conflict with our faith. Those feelings want to tell us who we are: that we have not proven ourselves to be God's children and therefore are not. Those feelings seem to speak more loudly than does our faith, which at times feels so irrelevant. Confessing our faith updates and strengthens the experience of our faith.

My story of faith began as a twelve-year-old and the first challenge I faced was spiritual self-doubt. Mine was a very definite conversion experience at an identifiable moment in time, so I can testify to its reality. Naturally, the early adolescent

years are packed with social pressures, hormonal volatil-
ity, and adolescent tensions related to the normal pursuit of
independence. There were times when I forgot who I became at
conversion and felt the pressure to conform to the expectations
and temptations the world offered. I felt the pressure to conform
to that worldly mold every day. I did not feel the reality of
my conversion more than once a week at church during that
phase of life.

My feelings were daily urging me to advance in my
conformity to the world's youth culture. The thought of eternity
would periodically frighten me, and I questioned whether I
was prepared to face God "if I should I die before I wake."[36]
I doubted that God claimed me as His own child because my
feelings insisted that I belonged to the world and should behave
accordingly. Amid all of the struggles I had with the various
temptations to sin, only a seldom feeling told me that I was a
Christian on the way to heaven. When I listened to my feelings,
I became more vulnerable to temptation and less sure of my
identity as a heaven-bound child of God.

The truth was that I had become a Christian and God did
claim me as His child. But the feelings produced by the mere
struggle with worldly pressure shouted the opposite to my
soul. The truth is that God was holding on to me during the
turbulent teens even if I did not feel His grip, for "...though
he stumble, he will not fall, for the LORD upholds him with
his hand" (Psalm 37:24). In fact, God's grip on me was much
tighter than my grip on God. Yet, my feelings did not tell me
anything about that truth.

Eventually I learned to confess my faith daily, first through
songs. My doubts could easily have discouraged my resolve to
follow Christ and been the impetus for an eventual rejection of
the faith. The songs that provided the remedy were not ones
that fit my preferred style of music, but were ones which words
enabled me to confess my faith. Among those songs was Bill

and Gloria Gaither's "Bethlehem, Galilee, Gethsemane," which lyrics recount the key events in the life of Jesus and each one followed by the refrain, "I believe. Yes, I believe."[37]

That refrain, along with other songs, reaffirmed what I believed to be true, and that repeated confession overcame my socially induced self-doubt. Confession of our beliefs is an ally to our faith that has been relied upon since the first-century church.

Later I confessed the truths of the faith by reciting scriptures of God's promises and assurance. I also learned how to recount the story of my own conversion. By confessing the truths found in God's Word and the truth of my personal conversion experience, my faith eventually corrected my feelings. In time, my feelings began to agree with my faith because they were taught to function as designed: to follow. Indeed, living according to the Truth did become easier when my feelings followed my faith.

My experience is common among growing Christians.

Adults are not prone to doubt because of the pressure of peers, but often succumb to doubt because of the disappointments of life. As the outcomes of our life fail to match our initial hopes and dreams, the questions about God resurface. For example, when children don't follow the parent's Christian faith, the parent is apt to face an age-old feeling of failure and he or she requires a fresh resolve. When health breaks or a child is born with a physical malady and prayers for healing seem unanswered, the suffering Christian faces the voice of doubt about God's ability to answer prayer in the first place. In times like these, confessing the tenets of our belief and the story of Jesus, renews our personal faith.

GRUDGES ARE DOUBTS THAT CAN BE OVERCOME

Recurring grudges are nothing more than our doubts about whether God has grown forgiveness in our soul. Those grudges are like other such doubts, for they are feelings that must be aligned with the truth. We experience God's growth through stages one through four and now we must face the challenge of doubt. We will overcome that doubt in the same way we overcome doubts about the reality of God or the certainty of our salvation. We must confess what is true.

Feelings of grudge linger because the reminders of the offense continue to surround us. The temptation to rehearse the hurt causes us to feel the grudge. We become alarmed at the feeling and question whether we ever did forgive the person. We doubt whether the act of forgiveness was authentically transacted. One cannot prevent feelings of a grudge from time to time. The objective is to avoid holding the grudge. Feeling is fleeting but holding the grudge etches a ruinous habit in our character; therefore, we must overcome feelings of grudge quickly.

Confessing the truth will quell the voice of those feelings of grudge. The truth is that we did forgive by faith as an act of our will. We forgave definitely at an identifiable moment of time. Forgiveness was accomplished because God worked it in us and we acted upon it. The feeling of grudge is merely an errant one that has been screaming too loudly.

We can overcome the feeling of grudge by confessing, "I did forgive _____ for what was done to me, and God accomplished that forgiveness in me." As often as the feeling of grudge surfaces, the confession of this truth must correct it. Whenever we are tempted to rehearse the hurt, we must answer by recalling the truth about the forgiveness transaction. Nothing about our act of forgiveness was incomplete. The problem lies in the fact that for too long, we have allowed our feelings to speak erroneously and loudly. Confessing the truth will realign our feelings.

Lingering grudges cannot be left uncorrected. Grudges can open the wound of bitterness and create a whole new problem in our soul. Harboring ill will is not a casual concern because it prevents us from loving each other "deeply from the heart" (1 Peter 1:22). Bitterness, like the offense itself, threatens the survival of any relationship.

THE POWER OF TANGIBLE ACTION

The more definite we make our act of forgiveness, the easier it will be to recall and confess it as truth. For that reason, stage four is best achieved by writing out our forgiveness when a face-to-face reconciliation is not a realistic possibility. A written statement of forgiveness functions like water-baptism after a personal conversion to Christ. We may not remember the details of the day and hour of our conversion, but we will remember our baptism because we got wet. Our baptism was tangible. Likewise, a definite and identifiable act of forgiving aids us in confessing the truth. This definite, tangible act is an antidote for the feelings of grudge. Aided by the tangibility of our act of forgiveness, we can respond to the feelings of resentment about the offense with the words of Clara Barton, related earlier in this book: "I distinctly remember forgetting it."

Do not be discouraged when feelings of grudge reappear. God has achieved stages one through four, which is evidence that God is growing forgiveness in our soul. The one who "began that good work will carry it on to completion" (Philippians 1:6). God will not quit and neither should we.

12

The Sixth Stage of Forgiveness: Re-labeling

Lord, let me see what you see.

FORGIVENESS HAS THE power to remove the label that marks a person as an offender. When a sin is removed, so is the label. In the absence of that label, forgiveness allows grace to affix a new one. Instead of being branded by a past failure, grace provides a new seal of a promising future. To finish the work of forgiving another, we ask the Lord for grace to mark the person by a positive, future possibility: *Lord, let me see what you see.*

THE SAINT FAMILY

The Christian has already experienced a renaming by God's grace. The brand each person wears prior to experiencing Christ as Savior is "sinner." The label "sinner" is a family name. We are born into the Sinner family, of which Adam is the head, and by our actions we confirm that we really do belong.[38] When

God forgives us, the title of "sinner" is removed and God's grace re-labels us with a new family name, "saint." "Saint" is the biblical label for those who have received Jesus Christ as Savior and Lord![39]

The word saint points to who the Christian is becoming. That biblical title points to the possibilities of our future. The Christian may not always perform like a saint or feel like one; nonetheless, it is the new label that God has affixed on the Christian. The label of saint is a "crown placed over our heads that for the rest of our lives we are trying to grow tall enough to wear."[40] The name saint continuously reminds the Christian of the new family membership, the new character quality, and the new victory over sin that is presently possible because of Christ.

When Christians refer to themselves as sinners, they are refusing to wear the label grace has given. The Bible never refers to the follower of Christ as a sinner and neither should we call ourselves that. When we use the wrong name, we tend to fulfill its meaning. Sometimes, Christians have called themselves sinners as a way of excusing or even justifying repeated sin.

It is with humility and a bit of fear that a Christian identifies with the new name of saint. The Christian knows that there is disparity between the reality of life in this world and the name saint, which only heaven bestows. A life in the throes of temptation does not feel very saintly. Yet, the name saint motivates the Christian to "take hold of that for which God has called us heavenward in Christ Jesus" (Philippians 3:14).

Referring to ourselves as saints, which also calls us heavenward, is God's design. We tend to live up to the name we are called. A family name of good repute keeps calling the family members to become good citizens. An honorable surname has been motivation for many wayward youth to become responsible adults. Our name reminds us who we really are.[41] The reminder of the Christian's holy name motivates us to overcome temptation.

FORGIVENESS AND RE-LABELING

God re-labels us as saints after forgiving our sin, and the renaming completes the forgiveness transaction. In the same way, a similar re-labeling of the forgiven offender completes the process of forgiving that person. When forgiveness stops short of a positive stamp on the forgiven, old grudges are more likely to resurface in our thought life. Grace re-labels a person and allows forgiveness to finish its work permanently.

Christians make forgiveness more difficult when the right is claimed to use the old stamp of "offender." The feeling of spiritual superiority deceives us when we see a person whom we have pardoned and identify them as "the person whom I forgave some years ago." Labeling such a person by the fact of our mercy is a way of identifying them with a sin. Furthermore, when we label a person by a forgiven offense, we leave ourselves open to be reminded of it.

Instead of labeling people by our forgiveness of their offense, grace labels them by their potential to bless us. Grace sees the forgiven one and identifies him or her as "the person who serves our church so well" or "the person who is wonderfully gifted by God." Better yet, grace enables us to re-label the one we forgave as "the brother/sister in Christ whom I love." In order to re-label a person whom we had previously identified with an offense, we must pray, "Lord, let me see what you see." We pray that prayer regularly as we trust God to change our view of the one we are forgiving.

A CONVERTED POINT OF VIEW

My story in chapter eight about the other driver whom I believed had lied about the damages continued beyond the initial forgiveness. The decision to forgive her was made definite for me one day as I was driving on some errands, but God continued growing a more complete forgiveness. When

I think of that driver, I no longer think of the event that first introduced us.

Over the course of three years, a total transformation took place. The fact that she worked with the elderly in a nursing home was noted because I would make visits to that facility. One time I saw her in the grocery store, loaded with enough groceries and other kinds of necessities to provide for a whole group. I recalled the disabled individuals who lived in her home, whose social security income I judged was being employed to purchase the nice furnishings for her home. I realized that her shopping trip included provisions for those disabled housemates.

Initially I resented that she would take advantage of the disadvantaged ones' income. That negative view of her under-went a conversion. I began to view her as a person without whom our community would be worse off. She was taking care of the sadly neglected elderly in our town. She provided a dignified home for some of our community's hopeless and likely homeless. Yes, she had been dishonest with me, but she practiced mercy in a manner superior to my own and that of my church. I began to admire her and what she does with her life. She works hard, is always under time-pressure, and never stops taking care of people. She never admitted anything to me, though the evidence is clear, but I have been humbled by my lack of mercy to the needy in comparison to hers.

She is a good person in our community, though flawed like all of us, and forgiveness allowed me to see her that way. Forgiveness was completed when I did view her differently, but the process of changing my viewpoint took time. When I see her now, I thank God that we have a person like her living in our community for the benefit of others, even if those others don't include me. The facts of our initial encounter do not ruin my respect for how she lives. With me, she bears a new label and God grew that more gracious view.

The Sixth Stage of Forgiveness: Re-labeling

This re-labeling more permanently removes the old grudges from our thoughts. For example, instead of thinking of the hard-nosed boss as selfish and insensitive, we can begin to recognize how his responsibility for everyone requires him to adhere strictly to policies. Making an exception for us might not have been so simple a matter as we first considered. Even though we would have preferred him to show a little respect during the encounter, we realize that we may have been at the tail end of several requests for an exception to some rule that day. Therefore, we re-label him as tough but fair, which fosters a much more agreeable working environment for both the boss and us.

A shift in viewpoint has the great potential of effecting a positive change in another individual's relationship to us. When one freshly divorced man re-labeled his ex-spouse as "a great mother with whom he wanted his children to spend equal time," he increased the likelihood that she might honor that trust and return the favor.

People tend to live up to the labels we give them. People tend to live up to their names, even the names that are never spoken but only felt.

POSITIONS OF LEADERSHIP AND TRUST

Re-labeling a person according to grace always keeps us open to new and godly possibilities that may grow in the one forgiven. However, re-labeling does not always mean restoring individuals to old positions, particularly ones involving the trust of leadership. It is possible to become disqualified for a role of leadership in ministry. The apostle Paul guarded himself against that possibility, "...so that after I have preached to others, I myself will not be disqualified for the prize" (1 Corinthians 9:27). Paul states the standard, which must be upheld regarding positions of trust when he says, "Now it is required that those who have been given a trust must prove faithful" (1 Corinthians 4:2). Likewise, the trust necessary to sustain a marriage can be broken even beyond the possibility of full reconciliation, or else God would not have permitted divorce in specific instances (Matthew 19:9). Even if we may not always be able to live with a situation, forgiving others will prevent hurtful situations from living in us.

The good news is that grace always restores a Christian person to a position of church fellowship by re-labeling that individual, as God did for each of us. The highest position in the church is that of God's child. When the church forgives, the greatest work of grace is the restoration to a position of fellowship and recognition as a child of God. Even when leadership trust cannot be restored, the place of loving fellowship can be when we forgive.

COMPLETING THE GROWTH

We can be confident that our forgiveness of another is complete when we have re-labeled the forgiven. However, there is a residual responsibility in forgiving, from which we are never fully released. In addition to accepting the new, positive label, we must always refuse the old one. We can always be tempted to associate that person with the past offense. That temptation is strongest if the person again offends us or another person. At that time we will be tempted to keep score, but love "keeps no record of wrongs"[42] and the temptation to do so must be refused. A new offense will certainly produce a fresh disappointment but need not refresh the old one. We have that choice. Refusing to use old labels after we have pardoned the offender requires the work of the Holy Spirit within the believer.

We ourselves become gracious people when we re-label the person we forgive according to the good things we choose to notice in that person. As we grow in such grace, we become like Christ. In so doing, we will find that forgiving others is a more-ready response because we are being conformed to Jesus' character. He is the one who forgave his offenders even while He hung on the cross. He refused to label people by their actions, for He chose to see something in the crowd, those soldiers, and the religious leaders that made Him sure that they were unaware of what they were really doing.[43]

This re-labeling has the power to bless all those around us. People are attracted to those who are gracious in their judgment of others. Everyone longs for a generous word to be spoken. We are already surrounded by reminders of our past failures and everyone needs grace. We long for a label of mercy and that is what God enables Christians to offer the world. Jesus conferred that ability to be gracious: "Receive the Holy Spirit. If you forgive anyone his sins, they are forgiven; if you do not forgive them, they are not forgiven" (John 20:22b-23). Forgive others to the point of re-labeling, and that same measure will be used in the way you are treated by God. "For in the same way you judge others, you will be judged, and with the measure you use, it will be measured to you" (Matthew 7:2). Each Christian is endowed with the authority to forgive to the point of re-labeling and in so doing, he or she will be recognized as a child of God. "Be merciful, just as your Father is merciful" (Luke 6:36).

SECTION THREE

HELP
FOR THOSE WHO
FORGIVE

13

How Much Time Will Forgiveness Take?

FORGIVENESS TAKES AS much time as grace does to change us. No clock or calendar is useful for gauging a time frame of forgiving another person. Progress is dependent upon the willingness and faith of the offended party throughout the six stages. The Christian's willingness to relinquish revenge determines the resistance or responsiveness to the Holy Spirit's work through the six stages of forgiveness.

MARKING SPIRITUAL GROWTH

Responsiveness to the Holy Spirit's movement is a measure of spiritual maturity. Paul encourages the Galatians toward maturity in the life of the Spirit by saying, "Since we live by the Spirit, let us keep in step with the Spirit" (Galatians 5:25). The Holy Spirit always grows forgiveness in us so that we can work it out to others (Philippians 2:13).

As we increase our readiness to respond to the Holy Spirit, less time is required for each stage of forgiveness. A good measuring stick for spiritual growth is how much time each stage demands in comparison to an earlier point in life. I was able to determine the progress of my growth in the grace of Christ, because forgiving someone's antagonistic remark about my ministry, which once claimed two weeks, required only two hours several years later. I long for the day when I will be able to forgive offenses almost immediately after they are experienced. Jesus did just that. While on the cross, Jesus said, "Father, forgive them, for they do not know what they are doing" (Luke 23:34).

It is my observation that the type of offense often determines the pace at which the forgiver moves through the stages. There are no categories of offenses and no timetables to consult that would indicate an estimated time for growing forgiveness. Clearly, the offenses that undermine our most personal identity take the longest time to forgive. For example, an insult inflicted upon a woman's intellectual achievement may be difficult to forgive, but an insult to a woman's motherhood tends to be more so. An act of disrespect to a man's athletic competence may be difficult to forgive, but it's much harder to forgive disrespect of his sexual capability.

An insult to us requires a work of grace to forgive, but an insult to our children tends to require a deeper work of the Spirit in the parent's soul. After all, parents are wired to defend their children rather than forgive those who hurt them. Our upbringing, childhood experiences, oft-repeated hurts, rejections, and ethnic or racial discrimination are factors that determine how deeply something hurts. These factors also play a part in which kinds of offenses will take the most time to forgive.

The need for more time never implies that forgiveness is impossible. God's grace is absolutely sufficient to forgive any hurt or offense. If the grace of God can forgive the sins of the whole world, it is sufficient for every believer who is willing to forgive any offense. The time frame for the six stages of forgiveness may vary, but it never calls the possibility of forgiving into question.

As our responsiveness to the Spirit increases, we will find the stages of forgiveness much less conflicted and the temptation for revenge much less enticing. However, no stage can be bypassed or treated superficially. Each stage must be experienced authentically and can be when we rely on the grace of Christ.

This does not mean the stages should be regarded as steps of action, for then we make them subject to our human achievement. They are stages of growth that the Spirit produces and to which we must respond. We must be careful not to run ahead of that authentic process. The temptation will surface to hastily declare that we are finished with any one stage of forgiveness before it is genuinely completed. A superficial process instead of an authentic growth results in a failure to finish. Grudges will continue to plague the one who has not truly grown in pardoning grace.

While forgiveness is being grown in stages, the believer's focus must remain on simply trusting and obeying, yielding and believing, rather than on what is being accomplished in each particular stage. The stages will emerge in the life of a fully surrendered, fully obedient Christian. Authentic growth is recognized in stages but is not produced because of one's knowledge of them. Recognizing the stages assures us but doesn't cause us to grow them more quickly. Our faith in the matter of forgiving others is not a matter of better insight but of remaining yielded and obedient.

Forgiveness is a part of the fruit of the Spirit's work even as love and kindness are. The fruit rests on the vine in a yielded state. No grape ever worried about its eventual success; it simply waited for the nutrients of the vine to produce its growth. That is how the Christian should rely on the Spirit of Christ (Romans 8:9). Spending over twenty years as pastor of one church requires people to forgive me and I them. The forgiveness is evidence that the Holy Spirit has been free to work among us. We are not unusual Christians. Experiencing this type of grace is promised to every church.

URGENT: FORGIVE NOW

The time needed to authentically grow forgiveness must never force the believer to a superficial experience, but that does not mean forgiveness is not urgent. The urgency is not to grow forgiveness at a faster rate than is real, but to begin before we lose someone permanently. There is a point in time at which it is too late to forgive and still experience the blessing of reconciliation. The opportunity when those relationships can be healed and restored might time-out before we realize that forgiveness was actually possible. Relocation, divorce, remarriage, law, damage, and death can nullify the possibility of reconciliation.

Reconcilable relationships can become inaccessible if we procrastinate. In the course of ministry, I have seen someone seek for a sign of reconciliation from a comatose brother with whom no word or even a glance had been exchanged for over twenty years. There was no response and the coma only gave way to death. The brother's desire for reconciliation was acted upon too late. If we wait too long to grow forgiveness, we may very easily be left with regret for the rest of our lives. It is urgent to begin the process of forgiveness even if it takes months to mature.

While forgiveness cannot be a superficial experience, the urgency is imperative for those who have forged the most intimate bonds. There are some threats to close relationships that can only be resolved by merciful pardon.

Most offenses in marriage simply cannot be compensated, so forgiveness is particularly critical. Only forgiveness, not FTD, can enable the marriage to keep growing or to begin healing after an insult, betrayal, or long-term neglect. He hurt her publicly with another thoughtless quip. He cannot take it back or make it up to her because once spoken, words have a life of their own. Only forgiveness will extinguish the flame of those ill-chosen words and mollify their edge. She can place him on probation but time will not heal the hurt; only forgiveness holds the cure and time is wasting away. The relationship will grow worse and invite more suffering apart from absolution. The unthinkable prospect of divorce will become a subject of secret thoughts. If forgiveness is not applied, the offending spouse will, at best, be placed on a repayment plan that will never be completed even with a lifetime of perfect behavior. Without forgiveness, the deficit will always exist and store a very deep, private fear in the heart of the penitent spouse. The marriage cannot progress well in a state such as this.

Withholding forgiveness in marriage is a form of revenge and control. Keeping a spouse in a debtor's prison may be thought to prove the so-called innocent party's moral excellence. It certainly gives the innocent one the control in the household. But there is no healing, no marital joy, and no grace until the offended party forgives. Forgiveness is imperative, no matter how long its time frame.

Forgiving others by the grace that God works in us is not only possible but is preferable. It is a tragic waste of life to dedicate one's energies to repaying the other party for an offense. No one is stronger for prospering at revenge, no matter how successful. Revenge is to strength what lust is to love, and the first negates the second in both cases. Forgiveness requires the power of God in us but revenge siphons the energy of life. Forgiveness is preferable, no matter how much time is needed for its full growth. For the one who buckles under the fear of failing at mercy, there is scripture's assurance that God will produce the forgiveness in our lives: "The one who calls you is faithful and he will do it" (1 Thessalonians 5:24).

14

The Preemptive Strike of Forgiveness

D O YOU WANT to apologize first or forgive first?" That was the question I asked a married person who was hurt deeply but didn't want a divorce. The hurt was deep but was not a ground for divorce, though that possibility had been considered. Because divorce was not an option for that Christian's marriage, only two possibilities existed if any marital satisfaction would be achieved: apology first or forgiveness first. There are nearly no marital breakdowns in which the fault is entirely one-sided. The first step toward healing a hurt marriage is to offer either an apology or forgiveness. Since we are far more likely to notice another person's fault before we do our own, forgiving becomes the first essential ingredient in cultivating a great marriage. Forgiving even before receiving an apology is a preemptive strike against the enemy of marital unity: unresolved conflict.

You First!

Wouldn't it be nice if people apologized to us as soon as they offended or betrayed us? Dream on; that's not reality. Forgiveness is required even in the absence of an apology. No statement in the Bible commands us to forgive only those who apologize to us. However, the Bible repeatedly commands us to forgive the ones who grieve or sin against us.[44] Forgiveness is commanded because someone has wronged us, not because they have apologized to us. Forgiveness that is contingent upon an apology is a worldly standard for relationships, not a gracious one. An unbeliever may offer forgiveness in exchange for an apology, but God's grace is required to forgive without receiving an apology.

Jesus taught both responsive forgiveness and preemptive forgiveness. "If your brother sins, rebuke him, and if he repents, forgive him. If he sins against you seven times in a day, and seven times comes back to you and says, 'I repent,' forgive him" (Luke 17:3-4). In this instance, Jesus teaches unlimited forgiveness for the one who repents and seeks it from us. Generally, the apology loses its impact after the fourth instance on the same day, and after that, we forgive by grace alone.

Jesus' whole teaching on the subject of forgiveness, however, does not limit forgiveness to cases where the offender repents. He taught forgiveness for others as a requirement for approaching a Holy God in prayer, without mentioning a prior apology. "And when you stand praying, if you hold anything against anyone, forgive him, so that your Father in heaven may forgive you your sins" (Mark 11:25). Again, Jesus teaches that our forgiveness is triggered by another's sin against us, not by an apology. "For if you forgive men when they sin against you…" (Matthew 6:14).

Jesus forgave His torturers preemptively in the very epicenter of His pain and humiliation on the cross. While He was in agony and the soldiers were gambling for His clothes, He initiated forgiveness. It is the very character of the Holy God to initiate forgiveness and reconciliation even before people acknowledge need for it. "While we were still sinners, Christ died for us" (Romans 5:8). Such a preemptive forgiveness cost God dearly. Forgiveness is never effortless or without a price to pay.

Spirit-Filled Forgiving

Nobody is able to forgive preemptively apart from the filling of the Holy Spirit. Forgiving each other as the Lord forgave us requires the fullness of the Holy Spirit and the death of our responsiveness to worldliness. In Ephesians, Paul summarizes this exchange of governing forces in our life by simply saying, "Be filled with the Spirit" (Ephesians 5:18).

Apart from the filling of the Spirit, none of the qualities of God's chosen, loved, and sanctified people are possible. But by yielding to the Spirit, all of the clothing of the Christ-like life becomes tailored to our lives. Colossians 3:12-13 says, "Therefore, as God's chosen people, holy and dearly loved, clothe yourselves with compassion, kindness, humility, gentleness and patience. Bear with each other and forgive whatever grievances you may have against one another." Forgiveness is the culmination of Christ-like living and most identifies with Jesus. "Forgive as the Lord forgave you. And over all these virtues put on love, which binds them all together in perfect unity" (Colossians 3:14).

Paul wrote the words about forgiving one another in the context of an exchange of our response to worldly enticement for a life in response to the Spirit's rule:

Put to death, therefore, whatever belongs to your earthly nature: sexual immorality, impurity, lust, evil desires and greed, which is idolatry… Let the peace of Christ rule in your hearts, since as members of one body you were called to peace. And be thankful. Let the word of Christ dwell in you richly as you teach and admonish one another with all wisdom, and as you sing psalms, hymns and spiritual songs with gratitude in your hearts to God.

—Colossians 3:5, 15-16

The Spirit enables us to forgive as the Lord forgave us, preemptively. This type of forgiveness is not a part of our earthly nature, which is always inclined toward revenge. Preemptive forgiveness is God's nature, in which people are called to participate.[45] This is not so much a demand as a promise we dare not refuse! That promise of forgiving preemptively as God forgave will save our marriages, churches, friendships, and places of work. Preemptive forgiveness is the gift of God to each believer and is a birthright for each Christian.

Close Relationship Requires Preemptive Forgiveness

Amperage measures how much electricity flows through a conducting wire. The gauge of the wire determines how much amperage will be tolerated before overheating and combusting. The electricity is like the relationship between two people who have a burning love for each other, and that flow of power contains potential conflicts, hurts, and offenses. Forgiveness must be in place before a burning love begins so that one may survive the close connection. A burning love without a forgiving heart is too much amperage for the gauge of the wire that connects the two people. Like the gauge of the wire, forgiveness determines our tolerance of that power. The gauge of the wire must be ample before plugging in to a power source, and preemptive forgiveness must be in place before engaging in a close relationship.

A burning love for another will bring one into an extremely close relationship and renders our personal identity vulnerable. That person, however, is part of a flawed humanity and is in need of forgiveness. The closer the relational bond, the greater the likelihood of conflict, hurt, and offense.

The dream of meeting the one who will never hurt us remains a fairy-tale. People who love us will always hurt us to some degree because no human knows another omnisciently nor loves absolutely. All of us are flawed human beings. Even if the man is charming and sensitive, he will fail. Even if the woman seems to care like no one else ever has, she cannot anticipate every emotional need at every given moment. Only a preemptive forgiveness will enable any close relationship to continue to flourish. Apart from preemptive forgiveness, the relationship will most certainly approach a point of destructive conflict; therefore, a close relationship with the object of our burning love will catch fire with conflict unless there is an ample tolerance made possible by forgiveness.

REGRET-FREE LIFE

People accumulate many regrets. Most of the deepest regrets are ones related to an unforgiving heart. For example, a rebound relationship is usually associated with an unforgiven rejection and leads toward moral regret. A person reacts to a rejection by becoming involved in a relationship outside of God's will just to prove worthiness or attractiveness. The reactive or rebound relationship usually results in a moral failure. Had forgiveness been applied first, the urge to react would have been doused. The worst consequence of the failure to forgive, whether preemptively or responsively, is the loss of relationship with those we really do love. Apart from forgiveness, love will not survive and we will live with the regret of its loss.

God's command to forgive is, in fact, a gift that preserves love. Preemptive forgiveness allows love to grow without interruption. Even in divorce, forgiveness is needed or the post-divorce life will be filled with difficulty. By commanding preemptive forgiveness, God is trying to make our lives easier, because regrets make life harder.

15

God's Transforming Forgiveness

WE WILL NEVER forgive others until we know the absolute forgiveness that comes only from God. The increase of civil litigation in America is evidence of a greater desire for profiteering from another's error than for pardoning it. Some parents, who may believe that revenge assures survival, are known to instruct their school-age children to 'hit back.' Teachers have their hands full of relational class-conflict because of a merciless culture. This is a symptom of an unforgiven society. Forgiveness will breed mercy but guilt will engender ruthlessness, for guilt is a harsh, dehumanizing tormentor. We are all members of a society that is becoming depraved because there is no mercy. We are all part of a humanity that needs forgiveness. We cannot be considered humane without it.

The good news in the Bible is the announcement that the needed forgiveness is provided by God. This pardon is made possible because of the greatest love known in history. God has made forgiveness available to all and is able to transform us into a merciful society. The following is a brief summation of the Bible's message of grace. It may serve as a refresher for the reader or it may be the missing link to a forgiving heart.

GOD INITIATES FORGIVENESS

But God demonstrates his own love for us in this:
While we were still sinners, Christ died for us.

—Romans 5:8

Forgiveness was God's idea. God initiated the forgiveness that reconciles us to Him. The blessings of being God's child were absent from our life because sin separated us from God. God created us with the benefits of nature's beauty, natural resources, family, good government, and the prevenient work of the Holy Spirit. Those benefits are inherited because all people were created in the image of God. Those advantages are given for earthly life so that a person must conclude from the evidence in nature that God is a holy, sovereign, loving, and charitable eternal Father.[46] On that basis, all people may claim to experience God as part of creation but that does not mean that all people are children of God. The blessings of earth belong to all of God's creation but the blessings of heaven belong only to God's children (Ephesians 1:3).

God loves us and we bear His image. God's love is a perfect love but this does not guarantee an automatic relationship. Being loved by God means that God comes seeking to reconcile us to Himself but that love still requires a response from people.

GOD PROVIDES FORGIVENESS THROUGH JESUS

The sin that separated us from the blessings for God's children is far more serious than our conscience ever dares to admit. The act that God calls sin is only a reflection of our rebellion against God's authority. "We all, like sheep, have gone astray, each of us has turned to his own way…" (Isaiah 53:6). Our acts of sin would not have occurred unless we had first rejected God's place of power over our lives. It is quite common to remain religiously active but reject God's value system and purpose for living. Church membership or personal spiritual interest cannot compensate for a personal rejection of God's authority. When we reject God's direction or neglect God's word for us, we reject God.[47] God cannot be something other than Lord to us, for that is who He is. Though people want God to be active in their lives for sentiment or protection, God cannot relate to us as His children unless we acknowledge His authority over us.

Our rejection of God's authority was disastrous. The rejection caused a split that only widened with time. Quickly God became a stranger and then an enemy to people. Once sin separated humanity from God, our independent attitude grew strong and people began to create their own idolatrous ideas about God and about sin.[48] People insisted on relating to God on their own terms. However, God is not subject to our terms of relationship; therefore, God remained absent from people's lives except by the indirect blessings of God in creation and through the prophets beginning with Abraham.

Without God, the soul dies, spiritually, morally, relationally and eternally. There are many kinds of death besides physical ones. We speak of death of a relationship, death of morality, and death of hope itself. These are symptoms of a death in our relationship to God. Ultimately this spiritual death will result in an eternal punishment called hell. Hell is the consequence of refusing God's place of authority in our lives and is the ultimate death; an eternal one. "They will be punished with everlasting destruction and shut out from the presence of the Lord and from the majesty of his power" (2 Thessalonians 1:9).

Sin kills and death was the consequence that fell on each person who has ever sinned. It is not as though this death would arrive eventually. Sin is killing us now. Morality, marriages, family relationships, friendships, national and international peace, and authentic spirituality began dying the moment sin was born in us.[49] Hell is the epitome of death by sin because it is the absence of all divine blessings. Hell is death by sin without a hope of redemption. Undoubtedly, this death is more than any person can afford to endure, either in this life or after.

God's love for those who bear His image seeks a remedy for such sin. "For God so loved the world that he gave His one and only Son, that whoever believes in him shall not perish but have eternal life" (John 3:16). How would God accomplish the transformation of a sin-sick, hell-bound humanity into a Spirit-filled, heaven-bound humanity? The answer is that God offered His Son, Jesus, as the substitute for us. Only Jesus is qualified to take the place of a sinful person because He, Himself, had no sin (2 Corinthians 5:21) and is eternal (Hebrews 13:8).

A QUALIFIED SUBSTITUTE

Jesus is eternally different from us in that, among other attributes, He is infinite and we are finite. That means that as an individual, I can only die for my own sin and not for another since I am limited to my own person. Because we are finite, each of us can only have our own physical, moral, and spiritual health and not another's. Nor can anyone have a personal relationship with God on our behalf, not even our parents, priest, or minister. Jesus, on the other hand, is unlimited in nature and therefore is not limited to Himself. He is able to be right with God on another's behalf and be sinful in another's place, and He was. "God made him who had no sin to be sin for us, so that in him we might become the righteousness of God" (2 Corinthians 5:21).

Jesus was without sin and is not personally obligated to pay the penalty of sin, for He was "tempted in every way, just as we are—yet was without sin" (Hebrews 4:15). His moral and spiritual perfection makes Him capable of substituting for our moral and spiritual imperfection. Jesus became the atoning sacrifice for our sin because only His sacrifice satisfies God's sin-free nature.[50]

Jesus' perfection can be imputed to all because He is both untainted by sin and unlimited by human nature though fully immersed in it. This is the miracle of the incarnation (Jesus' birth): God became human without ceasing to be God. Because of His eternal nature and flawless humanity, He is an able substitute for our penalty of sin and imputes His righteousness to our lives. God gave Jesus, His own Son, as the sacrifice that would be the sufficient substitute for the penalty of human sin. That penalty is death. God's love would not discard sinful people but would make a way for them to be reconciled to Him. God would provide the reconciling forgiveness.

OUR FAITH

A response of faith and repentance appropriates God's provision. As we said, there is an offer of forgiveness but not an automatic one. God's provision is so complete that it bestows the possibility of faith and repentance.[51] What do those words mean?

- Repentance means to turn from sin and self. Repentance is not a ritual confession but a reorientation of lifestyle. Repentance involves admission of sin and changing the values and purpose by which we live. Repentance is transformational because it directs our life God-ward and calls us to a godly lifestyle.

- Faith is trust to the extent of obedience to God. Faith means that I trust in the provision achieved by Christ crucified and resurrected to be sufficient for my forgiveness and reconciliation to God. But this trust is not merely agreement; it is involvement. Faith is expressed when two people exchange wedding vows and involves the whole person. Faith in Christ's provision for our forgiveness involves everything about us for as long as we live! The magnitude of such a decision gives character to the definition of faith as trust. When one thinks of faith, one should picture a wedding ring because marriage is an act of radical, life-altering faith in another person.

Faith and repentance are acts of our will that are expressed verbally in a prayer, but they are choices that involve our lives. When we place our faith in Christ, we pray a prayer of repentance and faith but nothing actually occurs unless we become followers of Christ. When we repent, we abandon a life that leads into sin and choose to live a life that leads into holiness. Repentance does not mean that upon the next occasion for sin, we will stop short of it; it means that the Christian will choose a different path altogether. Faith and repentance are a paired response to God's offer of transformation and reconciliation.

Expressing Faith

Prayer that expresses the desire of a person who is ready to repent and place faith in Christ always requires words. Words are only effective if they represent one's heartfelt desire. The words are not magical or formulaic; they can only express an act of our will to repent and believe. If the words do not represent our own desire and choice, they express nothing at all, regardless of their beauty. Many people desiring to repent and place faith in Christ have prayed a prayer similar to this one, and the reader is invited to do the same:

> *Lord Jesus, I need you. Thank you for dying on the cross for my sin.*
> *I ask you to forgive my sin and come into my life as my Savior and my Lord.*
> *I believe You rose from the dead and can change my life.*
> *Make me the kind of person you want me to be.*
> *Thank you.*

Dear reader, if you prayed that prayer as an act of repentance and faith, then you have been forgiven and reconciled to God. You received Christ and are a child of God. Revelation 3:20 says, "Here I am! I stand at the door and knock. If anyone hears my voice and opens the door, I will come in and eat with him, and he with me." John 1:12 says, "Yet to all who received him, to those who believed in his name, he gave the right to become children of God."

Now you are forgiven and are called to forgive others. A Christian pleases God most by offering forgiveness and reconciliation to others who have inflicted hurt. The forgiveness one receives with Christ makes one able to forgive others as well.

16

The First Order of Holiness: A Review

"Forgive us our trespasses as we forgive those who trespass against us."

—Matthew 6:12

W E MAY OR may not relate to the word *holiness*; however, we probably do value the word *forgiveness*. Who wouldn't want to be forgiven of one's offenses against God or people? The offenses of others and the resultant hurts threaten our spiritual purity with the temptation of bitterness. Bitterness makes us spiritually impure and unholy. Unholiness is precisely that for which we blame the offender, but when bitterness enters into the heart of the one hurt, both the offender and offended are made unholy.[52]

Forgiveness is the very first step into holiness. People want forgiveness for that which is unholy in their lives. This claim is shown to be true by the many appeals for mercy in relationships, religion, and law. Confronted with our own unholiness, we either seek forgiveness for it or simply deny it. Ultimately, people either desire forgiveness from God or else deny God's existence altogether as a way to reduce feelings of guilt.

The divine forgiveness that people value is not merely a shallow remedy for guilt. Forgiveness is always transformational. God's forgiveness transforms us from being full-of-sin to being full-of-holiness. If forgiveness were only a remedy for guilt, the removal of sin from our record of conscience and reputation, then it would do nothing more than neutralize our soul. But, a person who has been forgiven by God or another person is transformed from one estranged to one embraced. The forgiven person has a new vision for relationships, behavior, love, and faith. Forgiveness does not just produce a neutral state of the soul but fills us with holiness. Forgiveness transforms us from full of sin and separated from God into the righteousness of God (2 Corinthians 5:21).

PASSING ON THE GIFT

Such an exhilarating experience of true holiness has an immediate demand, that the one who is forgiven would also forgive others: *Forgive us our trespasses as we forgive those who trespass against us.* In the prayer that teaches about essential faith, forgiveness and forgiving are inseparably bound. Jesus yoked forgiveness and forgiving together, not because God is exacting payment, but rather that forgiveness and grudge-bearing are contradictions and cannot coexist in the same soul. Therefore the first order of holiness is the act of forgiving another.

We would like for the first order of holiness to be the elimination of our bad habits. We even offer God the eradication of our crude speech habits, the reordering of our schedule to include going to church, and the redirection of our life's purposes when we seek divine blessing. Our conversation with God will probably sound something like this:

The First Order of Holiness: A Review

We pray, "God, I'll give up smoking, drinking, drugs, porn, and gluttony."

But God responds with, "How about if we begin with forgiving your irresponsible parent, self-centered sibling, or arrogant coworker?"

We then retort, "Can we do that down the road?"

God answers, "No, forgiving others is the first order of the life that I bless and the first necessary response to being forgiven. We'll deal with your bad habits later."

THE FIRST SIGN OF GRACE

Knowing that the primacy of forgiving others would go right over the heads of His disciples, Jesus reiterated this first order of holiness. "For if you forgive men when they sin against you, your heavenly Father will also forgive you" (Matthew 6:14).

This first order of holiness is essential. It is impossible to sustain forgiveness and unforgiveness simultaneously. Jesus knew that they were mutually exclusive. While God's forgiveness of sin is the first step of our walk with Christ, our forgiveness of those who hurt us follow in stride. We must not think that God is withholding something good from us until we deliver something else for God. This is not about a deal God is making. The very nature of forgiveness demands that the forgiven become a forgiver. Forgiveness cannot coexist with grudge-bearing in our souls for very long, just as light and darkness cannot coexist. One will exclude the other.

The Lord's Prayer identifies forgiving others as the first ethical demand of God's grace. Forgiving others may not be the only moral requirement of holiness, but it ranks first because it is the one in Jesus' prayer primer. This fact shows us that forgiving others is ranked first on the agenda of the Spirit's sanctifying work. God's forgiveness is the entry into holiness, and forgiving others is the first step past the gate.

In Matthew's gospel, Jesus told a parable about a man who was deeply indebted to his employer (Matthew 18:23-35). As a manager, the man had taken personal liberties with company money. He was indebted up to his eyeballs and had no means of repayment, not even in a lifetime of trying.

The dreaded day of accounting came. The manager was caught and convicted and he needed mercy. The manager's employer forgave the suffocating debt and he was absolutely free. But the manager did not pass along that favor. He had also loaned some small amounts of money to his own colleagues. They needed only time in order to repay their debt and indeed were in the process of doing so. But instead of giving them the needed time, the manager sent some unscrupulous debt collectors and had those colleagues thrown into debtor's prison.

That action of the manager was not in keeping with the gift he himself had received. The gift of forgiveness came first and the new expectation of this state of freedom was the very opposite of retribution. As the story unfolds, the manager's own employer, who was so gracious to him earlier that day, heard about this inconsistent behavior. Because the forgiveness the manager received had not transformed him into a forgiving person, the initial forgiveness was withdrawn.

God's forgiveness is freely given, and our entry into holiness is entirely by God's grace. However, the next step we take in that "way of holiness" (Isaiah 35:8) is to be the act of forgiving others. Failure to forgive others amounts to a departure from "the Way" (Acts 9:2), and that is why forgiving others is the first order of holiness by God's grace.

POWER TO FORGIVE

Forgiving others is so vital to life in God's grace that Jesus made it the first recognizable sign of the kingdom of God. Jesus conferred upon His disciples the kingdom of God when He said, "And I confer on you a kingdom, just as my Father conferred one on me" (Luke 22:29). How will that kingdom authority be expressed? Consider John's account of the conferment of the kingdom after Christ's resurrection: "If you forgive anyone his sins, they are forgiven; if you do not forgive them, they are not forgiven" (John 20:23).

Today, Christians might think of the power of the kingdom of God only as it is expressed in dramatic physical healing, ecstatic uttering of an unknown heavenly language, or the winning of the culture war. These have their place in the history and future of the kingdom of God but are not the primary expression of kingdom authority on earth. The authority of the kingdom of God is expressed in the power to forgive others.

Jesus conferred upon His disciples the kingdom of God as a mission to bring forgiveness on earth. He sent them by saying, "Peace be with you! As the Father has sent me, I am sending you" (John 20:21). He empowered them when He breathed on them and said, "Receive the Holy Spirit" (20:22). He commissioned them to offer forgiveness, saying, "If you forgive anyone his sins, they are forgiven; if you do not forgive them, they are not forgiven" (20:23).

Notice that Jesus did not limit the power to forgive only to the eleven. The power of the kingdom of God to forgive was bestowed on all of the disciples upon whom the Spirit was breathed. There were assembled not just apostles, but also "those with them, assembled together" (Luke 24:33). Jesus referred to all Christians, even ones yet to come, when He said, "If you forgive anyone his sins, they are forgiven; if you do not forgive them, they are not forgiven." The power to forgive, authorized by Jesus, belongs to every Christian, for each is to obey everything Jesus taught the twelve apostles.[53]

THE MISSION OF FORGIVING

Each Christian has a significant power. If we forgive someone, that person becomes free from the guilt of the offense when the gift is received. We have the power to withhold forgiveness and tether a person with guilt. The choice to offer forgiveness or withhold it is in each Christian's hands. Anyone can withhold forgiveness but the Christian is divinely authorized to offer it on earth.

The Christian's mission, unless we refuse it, is to bring forgiveness on the earth. Jesus mandated and modeled it. Jesus has empowered Christians to fulfill that mission. Therefore, every believer has the birthright to offer forgiveness on earth and the world longs for the love which that offer holds.

Forgiving others is the first order of holiness and the most noted distinctive of the kingdom conferred upon the church. God makes forgiving others a real possibility and a gift of God's grace to each yielded believer. It is therefore a prerequisite for heaven itself. "For without holiness, no one will see the Lord" (Hebrews 12:14).

God will lead each one of His children to forgiving others as He prepares us for eternity. It may be one of the last items on God's agenda for our earthly life. Forgiveness was a crucial part of one friend's final earthly day. Tony was a wonderful Christian man who had been overcharged for some work. His coworker, Jeff, knew about incident and was with Tony on Friday, the last day of the work week. Whenever they would spot the man who had taken advantage of Tony, Jeff described how he loved to tease him as they rode together in the county-owned truck for the road department. Jeff tells the rest of the story as follows:

"I always teased Tony about it. We'd be going along the road and I'd nudge him and say, 'Hey, there's your buddy, Tony,' and he'd turn red in the face and get little aggravated and then get over it. We'd run across the guy almost every day. This went on for four months or so.

"Then one day as we were driving down Washington Avenue, I nudged him and said, 'There's your buddy, Tony.' He looked at me straight in the face. I realized that Tony knew *I* was having problems getting over a lot of stuff that had taken place in my life and it was affecting me.

"'You know, Jeff, I got to forgive him,' said Tony. Nothing else was said and he seemed so final about his decision.

"'Huh?' I said, a little startled by Tony's frankness.

"'Yeah, I got to forgive him,' Tony replied.

"That statement kinda shocked me because when Tony saw that guy, he'd get red in the face. In fact, just two weeks earlier, we were putting in a Culvert pipe for that guy and Tony told us on his crew, 'I'm not going out there.'

"Tony forgave the guy and the joke was over. It didn't come up the rest of the day. That conversation taught me that I needed to do some forgiving in my own situation. He forgave the guy the last day he was with us and I'll never forget it."

Tony suffered an entirely unexpected heart attack that night. He was forty-six and should have survived the ordeal but did not. God was leading and had grown forgiveness in Tony's soul, and it did not fail to bear fruit at the right time. He died at peace with people and prepared for eternity because Jesus was his Savior and he bore no grudge in his heart. "If you do not forgive men their sins, your Father will not forgive your sins" (Matthew 6:15).

Forgiveness is a priority on God's agenda for our earthly life. The act of forgiving others will lead us to seek God's mercy and sufficient grace in our own time of need.[54] For that reason, God amply pours out His Spirit. The pages of this book were intended to offer the blessing of forgiving others.

Endnotes

1. Vera Zwar, "A Tribute to Allan Littman 1959-1978," *The Baptist Herald* (a publication of the North American Baptist Conference), October 1978, 7.
2. Ibid., 9.
3. Dr. Charles Littman, "We've Picked Up The Pieces" (a personal testimonial written for friends and church members, courtesy of Audrey Littman, n.d.), 1.
4. Scott Williamson, "Jerome Wilson Not Positively Identified: Bank Tellers Testify In Market Murder," *The Herald-Palladium,* March 16, 1979.
5. Scott Williamson, "Judge Throws Key Away For Wilson," *The Herald-Palladium,* April 13, 1979.
6. Ibid.
7. Ibid.
8. Littman, op. cit.
9. Ibid.
10. Ibid., 2.
11. Ibid.

12. Audrey Littman, e-mail message to author, August 16, 2008.

13. Matthew 10:8.

14. Matthew 6:12.

15. Psalm 23:6.

16. 1 Thessalonians 5:24.

17. Luke 18:27.

18. Moody Bible Institute, Today in the Word (March 1989), 8.

19. John 10:10: "'The thief comes to kill, steal and destroy, but I have come that you might have life and have it to the full.'"

20. H. Jackson Brown, *Live and Learn and Pass It On, Volume II: People Ages 5 to 95 Share What They've Discovered About Life, Love, and Other Good Stuff* (Nashville: Rutledge Press, 1995), 86.

21. Matthew 6:34: "'Therefore do not worry about tomorrow, for tomorrow will worry about itself. Each day has enough trouble of its own.'"

22. M. Deutsch, "Justice and Conflict," in The Handbook of Conflict Resolution: Theory and Practice (San Franciso: Jossey-Bass, 2000), 52. Quoted in Dean B. Pruitt and Sung Hee Kim, Social Conflict: Escalation, Stalemate, and Settlement (3rd ed., McGraw Hill: New York, 2004), 54.

23. The rest of the stress-points are assigned to items that are death related or other life-changing experiences.

24. Bill Gothard, Institute in Basic Youth Conflicts: Research in Principles of Life (Institute of Basic Youth Conflicts, 1979), 24.

25. Psalm 73:21-22, "When my heart was grieved and my spirit embittered, I was senseless and ignorant; I was a brute beast before you."

26. We will not take up the purely philosophical question of omniscience and God's claim to not remember something. For now, it is sufficient to rely on the omnipotence of God

for the possibility of God remembering or purposefully not remembering and rely on faith to resolve the philosophical incongruence.

27. Clyde M. Narramore, *Encyclopedia of Psychological Problems* (20th Printing, 1980, Grand Rapids: Zondervan, 1966), 276.

28. Pruitt, op. cit., 218.

29. Paw Prints Anecdotes, http://pawprints.kashalinka.com/anecdotes/barton.shtml (accessed November 9, 2008).

30. Radio interview with Gordon Wilson in Sein Fein Atrocities, "The Enniskillen Remembrance Day Massacre," http://www.iraatrocities.fsnet.co.uk/enniskillen.htm (accessed June 8, 2009).

31. Phillip Yancy, *What's So Amazing About Grace* (Grand Rapids: Zondervan, 1997), 118.

32. *Spider-man 3.* dir. Sam Raimi, Columbia Pictures presents a Marvel Studios/Laura Ziskin production. Culver City, CA: Sony Pictures Industries, 2007, video recording.

33. Mark 16:18: "…they will place their hands on sick people, and they will get well."

34. Michigan State University Extension, "Fruit AOE Bud Stage Reference—Pome Fruit," http://web1.msue.msu.edu/fruit/pomegrw.htm (accessed June 8, 2009).

35. "…for it is God who works in you to will and to act according to his good purpose" (Philippians 2:13). "This is the confidence we have in approaching God: that if we ask anything according to his will, he hears us. And if we know that he hears us—whatever we ask—we know that we have what we asked of him" (1 John 5:14,15).

36. A common child's prayer at bedtime: "If I should die before I wake, I pray, dear Lord, my soul to take."

37. William Gaither, et al., "Bethlehem, Galilee, Gethsemane," sheet music (Alexandria, IN: Gaither Music Co., 1970).

38. Romans 5:12-17, esp. 14: "Nevertheless, death reigned from the time of Adam to the time of Moses, even over those who did not sin by breaking a command, as did Adam, who was a pattern of the one to come."

39. The title *Saint* is prevalent in the New Testament as a reference to Christians, which are represented by these references used in Ephesians 1:1, 15, 18; 3:18; 6:18.

40. Howard Thurman, *Words of Wisdom,* the Howard Washington Thurman National Memorial at Morehouse College, http://www.morehouse.edu/about/chapel/thurman_wisdom.html (accessed June 9, 2009).

41. "How great is the love the Father has lavished on us, that we should be called children of God! And that is what we are!" (1 John 3:1).

42. 1 Corinthians 13:5: "It is not rude, it is not self-seeking, it is not easily angered, it keeps no record of wrongs."

43. "Jesus said: 'Father, forgive them, for they do not know what they are doing.' And they divided up his clothes by casting lots" (Luke 23:34).

44. "Bear with each other and forgive whatever grievances you may have against one another. Forgive as the Lord forgave you" (Colossians 3:13). "Then Peter came to Jesus and asked, 'Lord, how many times shall I forgive my brother when he sins against me? Up to seven times?' Jesus answered, 'I tell you, not seven times, but seventy-seven times'" (Matthew 18:21-22).

45. "Through these he has given us his very great and precious promises, so that through them you may participate in the divine nature and escape the corruption in the world caused by evil desires" (1 Peter 1:4).

46. Psalm 19:1-4 and Romans 1:18-27.

47. 1 Thessalonians 4:8.

48. This is the message of Romans 1:18-32.

49. "...but each one is tempted when, by his own evil desire, he is dragged away and enticed. Then, after desire has conceived, it gives birth to sin; and sin, when it is full-grown, gives birth to death" (James 1:14-15).

50. "He is the atoning sacrifice for our sins, and not only for ours but also for the sins of the whole world" (1 John 2:2).

51. "But I, when I am lifted up from the earth, will draw all men to myself" (John 12:32). "When he comes, he will convict the world of guilt in regard to sin and righteousness and judgment..." (John 16:8).

52. Hebrews 12:14-15.

53. Matthew 28:20.

54. Hebrews 4:16.